I've travelled the world twice over,
Met the famous: saints and sinners,
Poets and artists, kings and queens,
Old stars and hopeful beginners,
I've been where no-one's been before,
Learned secrets from writers and cooks
All with one library ticket
To the wonderful world of books.

© **JANICE JAMES.**

ALL THE YEAR ROUND
An Allotment Diary

This allotment diary is definitely not a 'how-to-do-it' book, but rather a light-hearted record, based on a distillation of several years' entries, describing the work and inhabitants of a suburban allotment site. The author uses incidents and people as an excuse to recall events from her own childhood spent close by the site, which was then a great garden attached to the 'big house'. The allotments, situated near London (the plotholders prefer to say 'Kent'), provide a rich mixture of produce, wildlife and plot-people.

NELL BENNETT

◆

ALL THE YEAR ROUND

An Allotment Diary

Illustrations by Carol Walkin

Complete and Unabridged

ULVERSCROFT
Leicester

First published in Great Britain in 1992
in a shorter, illustrated edition by
The Mullet Press
Kent

First Large Print Edition
published November 1994
by arrangement with
The Mullet Press
Kent

British Library CIP Data

Bennett, Nell
    All the year round: an allotment diary.
    —Large print ed.—
    Ulverscroft large print series: non-fiction
    I. Title
    828.914

    ISBN 0–7089–3180–4

Published by
F. A. Thorpe (Publishing) Ltd.
Anstey, Leicestershire
Set by Words & Graphics Ltd.
Anstey, Leicestershire
Printed and bound in Great Britain by
T. J. Press (Padstow) Ltd., Padstow, Cornwall

This book is printed on acid-free paper

This book is a distillation of several allotment diaries. Some of the characters are modelled in part on plot-people, others are fictitious. All are regarded with affection.

for
TANTY
with love

January

Twelfth Night!

DEEP snow, bother! No chance of a good dig or even getting at the leeks and parsnips. Put on wellies when the snow stopped falling midday and walked up to the plot. Snow deep and soft, some already falling off the trees onto us.

Arrived to find not a soul there, not surprisingly. Mrs Somme's fruit cage had a great sagging underbelly of snow — hope it's weight won't bring it to the ground. Made the first footprints across the white car park. All the tool boxes, wheelbarrows, cabbages, piles of sticks had hats of snow. We shook them off the sprouts and picked a basketful. They were very cold and hard and will need quick cleaning and cooking or they'll go soggy and smelly. I had brought disposable gloves to put over my woollen ones . . . they worked well. I dropped

1

one as I was putting it on and there was enough light wind to pick it up, taking it almost the full length of the plot before I could catch it.

A robin joined us as we picked, very bright and perky. We walked back through the park for a change. There were lots of children tobogganing and building snowmen. The lake was only partially frozen but there was a good collection of icicles at the waterfall. When I was small the lake froze over really well one year and we were allowed to walk on it, a great excitement! It seemed odd to have a duck's-eye view of the park. We did not possess skates but slid about in wellies happily careering across the usually forbidden territory. It lasted for about a week and I do not think it ever happened again. When I see pictures of jolly goings-on in past centuries on the frozen Thames, I recall this childish memory quite clearly.

The aviary birds had all retreated inside and we hoped that they were warm enough. The dogwood was red and gold by the lower lake opposite the

2

wild bit, (near where the plots adjoin the park, up behind the trees) with it's usual seepage running right across the path towards the water, in an icy treacherous trail.

Sunday pm
Snow peppered down after we had been there half an hour or so but it didn't seem cold.

Soil quite softish under hard top layer so managed to dig up some good sized parsnips. Pulling leeks by hand is still risky so dug these up too. They are plumping up now.

Covered broad beans with PVC corrugated arches, a few were already blackened from snow but in the main are green and sturdy.

Wednesday
Met Winnie in Safeways, "Had we got her Christmas card?" . . . I had to admit that I did not think we had and when she told me that she had placed it up on our allotment in a plastic bag, tied to a raspberry stake, knew that we hadn't! Sure enough, there it was, a little cockled

from the winter damp but the message, belated through no fault of its own, still warm.

Heard today that our widower plotholder up near the flats is to remarry. After four years on his own we are glad for him. She is a "lady from Newcastle" so we all hope that she will like us "Southerners" and our funny ways! Imagine that she must be a keen gardener or she wouldn't be taking on Ted. Neither have children to approve or disapprove so good luck to them both.

Dug up parsnips, leeks and artichokes. Cooked the last and made a windy scented puree for a soup base.

Saw a fox saunter away into the park. Frost forecast.

Thursday
Went up for just an hour or so. Dull day, never lightened up properly. Got two wheelbarrows and forked chunks of leaf compost with some vigour as it was very cold and damp. Alf has made a really good job of the cache with posts and strong chain-link fencing. The Council has put in masses of local

leaves all through the autumn and they are already compacted and seem to be in a kind of strata. Hard to dislodge and James worked away with his larger fork while I gathered up the looser stuff. The leaf-mulch was all sticky, brown and black, warm to the touch and sweet-smelling, not unpleasant. It reminded me of giant tea leaves from a pot of Earl Grey!

★ ★ ★

Saw no foxes today but when we returned home a mangy one slunk across the lawns towards the fence while another, healthier-looking, more tan than grey (but still not as red as the country kind), went another direction beside one of the town houses. I expect this ill-assorted pair may well be the ones that wake us at night with their screeching and screaming as they fight, chasing each other up and down the neighbour's lawn — dark thrashing shapes, making their unholy din. Territorial rights I suppose but eerie, and sad too if the vanquished one is so sickly. Quite expect to find a muddy body in the lane later if not sooner.

Monday
Very heavy frost. Rimey twigs and the evergreen shrubs look really stricken and collapsed, but you have to be optimistic and just trust that they all will recover. Even the bergenia leaves look sad. Are they really called "elephant ears"? If so, they do indeed resemble them now!

No chance to dig up the polyanthus plants as planned as the ground is far too hard, too hard for digging up, too hard for planting in the border, they'll have to wait.

The water tanks were frozen over, quite thickly.

Percy remarked that he had heard that you should never turn the soil when there was a recent frost. None of us knew why exactly but it would be a hard task anyway. We talked about the old ice houses where ice blocks were kept for months under the soil "hat" roof. Maybe if you turned the frosty soil inwards by digging now, you delayed the warming process for early seed-sowing? Snow is

6

forecast again but there were clear skies over the plots at sunset . . . lavender in the East this morning, now lavender in the west tonight, matching ends to a blue and white day.

Tuesday
Bought a whole lot of seeds at the garden centre. Gather feverfew makes a good border plant as well as being a preventive for the migraine. Winnie says that it is very prone to blackfly but once established will seed itself for ever. I like the brightness of the foliage, more lime than leaf-green.

Keep on seeing even better onion sets, and bargains of seed potatoes, so getting far too many!

Wednesday
The whole house smells of brussels! It's not so bad when you know the origin. I have been blanching the morning's pick, we'll freeze the best and eat up the others or maybe blend them in with a current soup stock. Windy mixture! Phil came to tea later, with Daisy who was accused of making doggy-smells quite wrongly. She

7

looked injured and reproachful as only Dachshunds can!

February

Sunday, late afternoon

BRIEF visit to get leeks and parsnips. Had a go at a bonfire as the raspberry canes are quite twiggy, and the old cuttings from the gooseberry pruning seemed dry. Succeeded at second attempt so left a hat of damper stuff on top when we left.

There were several other bonfires around without their plotholders in evidence and the couple from the corner town house were there having quite a blaze.

We rarely see them in the wintertime as they are summer people, loving the sun more than the allotments, perhaps they ought to migrate? Anyway, he was the one who used to leap over the fence furious at our bonfires, threatening all sorts of things as the smoke drifted towards his house, but a persuasive Alf managed to get him to join us as a plotholder so now he is one of us. With the making of the combined combustible pile at the top of the site, there has been far less cause for complaint from any of the neighbouring householders, but as ever, it needs everyone to take note that individual bonfires are not encouraged and that all should use the common area. ("Can't the silly buggers read!" moans Alf).

Birdsong much more now both in quantity and volume.

Saturday
New horseradish shoots just appearing and we had to cover the bright green young rhubarb leaves yet again with beech-leaf compost. Wonder if there is more cold weather to come?

★ ★ ★

The plot seems to become smaller as it gets dug over, to shrink, an optical (optimistic?) illusion. Nearly all done now. Have unspiralled the old bean-stems but have left in the roots as this releases nitrogen into the soil. Went up to the shed to buy some seed compost. Overheard ratty man calling out "You need a driving licence . . . !" to a struggling plot-holder weaving his way up the narrow path with a load of compost bags on a porter's trolley. Said with uncalled-for irritation rather than with the more usual good humour found on the site.

When we first had a plot we were next to a man who was an accomplished gardener, amiable on the whole but larded his conversation to himself and all and sundry with four letter words, one in particular. After the initial shock, we affectionately christened him "effing-Fred". We missed him when he died and found his replacement, a rather quiet lady less entertaining albeit more restrained!

Tuesday
Chopped off the ends of the leeks with the spade and put the green ends in the trench but keep some green middle stalk for the soup pot. Only a few sprouts left on the top plot and the pigeons had somehow got underneath the protective

11

netting and shat all over the tops as they pecked them to shreds, destructive and messy! White fly still come off in clouds as you harvest the last of the crop, they seem to be great survivors. Will burn all the roots later because of club root disease.

The bonfire smoke was blue and multidirectional, eye smarting, painful. The sky was beginning to clear and the sounds too . . . an old single-engined aeroplane buzzing, some blue tits and the regular robin.

Left the bonfire now smelling pleasantly (to us if not the neighbours) of bubble and squeak!

Brought home parsnips, leeks and a few sprouts and a load of mud caught up in the tread of my gardening shoes. James cross with my trail of bits across the carpet . . . should have "changed them on the step" as he said.

Thursday
Terrible pong around our plots today. Turns out to be a load of chicken muck acquired by Ruth in a rash moment from a man with a "bargain". The smell

comes over in great waves, quite revolting which is strange as you would think that what chickens consume would result in something less unpleasant. I asked James as he has memories of homemade mashes concocted for their own hens in wartime. He remembers well, Mr Newbolt, a school teacher who lived two doors away from his family home who had a daughter who was described as "delicate". James never saw her properly as she was always swathed in scarves and heavy clothes, something of a mystery figure to a small boy. To supplement the frugal wartime food rationing, Mr Newbolt built quite a large construction in his garden where he kept chickens and rabbits, no doubt wishing to make his ailing daughter's diet a better one, their own too. His birds were kept in a kind of "battery", that is, boxes for each bird but they had a small run for exercise as well. The whole operation to James' admiring parents seemed very impressive and high tech', so not to be outdone they decided to do a smaller scale but similar operation. The posters urged "DIG FOR VICTORY" . . . "GROW YOUR OWN

13

FOOD" . . . so his family were not to be left behind in patriotism or good husbandry!

A hen-house was made from a collection of wooden egg boxes with windows cut out and covered with wire-mesh netting. In this modest environment they hoped that the hens would be happy and lay. Some roofing felt was scrounged from somewhere and a piece of chicken-wire to make a mini-run in the small garden. The first inhabitants were four Rhode Island Reds bought from the farm over at Keston and later they acquired a couple of White Sussex.

The birds were duly registered at the local Food Office and a license obtained for the purchase of balancer meal. (Two doors down from James' home lived Mr Jupp who held the most important job of "Food Officer" for their district, so it was very important to do everything correctly!).

The potato peelings and kitchen scraps were all boiled up together and then the dry precious meal was added, stirred in well. A treat for the hens was a little "real" corn but this was a rarity. It was a revolting-smelling concoction but the birds seemed to like it! Sometimes they had a supplement to their grey porridge diet in the shape of a cabbage, and had a great time leaping up at the suspended green leaves.

To "get them going" James recalls adding a red powder to their rations of mash called Karswood Spice or similar, something like a hen-type Vindaloo with much the same effect! Once his parents forgot to add the very necessary addition of grit to their feed and the hens produced soft-shelled eggs, disgusting! Having only the inner membrane the eggs splatted all over the floor at a touch and were cannabalised by the birds, the whole incident enough to put you off eggs for life!

A "sitting" of eggs was bought at one time, for a broody hen. These were hatched out successfully in spite of her being a bad mother, who soon stopped feeling broody and deserted them. However, with a succession of hot water bottles all were duly hatched and cossetted into young pullets and cockerels. More common was to slip a china egg under the broody hen as a substitute for the real thing. James reckoned that the nicest job then was the egg collecting, lifting the wooden outer doors to take out the warm brown eggs. Less popular was the cleaning out of the hen-houses particularly when there was a plague of mites. Evidently dust baths keep most pests away, but with a small run the birds were prone to such troubles and James and his brother had to take their turn at limewashing and scrubbing out.

Worse still was the attempt at killing one of their raised young cockerels. The bigger brother, full of do-and-dare made a bodge job of the slaughter and feeling a little sick, watched as the victim with a supposedly wrung neck, got to its feet and made off! It did die in fact but was buried not consumed. Always the sentimental attachment to James' family's feathered and furry friends proved too much, and not a single chicken or rabbit was eaten, inevitably becoming pets with names and proper personalities, never to grace their table. As to Mr Newbolt, maybe he was less squeamish, with his superior accommodation, incubators with light bulbs, all the trappings of a "proper" poultryman.

Saturday
The muck lady from the stables phoned to let James know that she had a load ready for him and Alf to collect.

"I've had a posse of landscape gardeners in" she told him, "lovely two-year-old vintage stuff exposed now, and lots of gravy!"

She recommended him to come over soon as "they" were returning in a week's time to get more. Alf is duly contacted and they arrange to take the van over to the stables soon to pick up the free goodies.

The rhubarb is breaking up through the beech-leaf mulch, you can almost see it grow! Brilliant greens and pinks. I must have a check on what old stock there is in the freezer still and clear it out before we start this years' harvesting. Time for a chutney session maybe. A happy discovery last week was to open a pot of what I thought was plum jam, only to discover that it was vintage rhubarb chutney, dark, sweet, sticky and delicious!

A less happy discovery happened last summer in connection with the freezer. We were two weeks away from visiting family in Germany and our chest freezer in the garage ground to a halt. It was brimful of produce and we panicked! It was a quite an age we knew but apart from seeming a little noisy of late, was in good order and had given no warning signs of imminent failure.

Phoning around, we soon learned that the local stores did not stock freezers of this size but could get one in a "few weeks". (It was only later that we learned that we could have contacted our High Street Freezer Centre which has a 24 hour replacement system, storing your stuff if wished while awaiting the new fridge. But we did want a particular make, so even if we had known this then, I don't think it would have solved our problem). Anyway, all was not lost as several of our kind neighbours helped us out with odd spaces in their own freezers, and Bill and Cissie, fellow plotholders, said that the chest freezer in their garage was nearly empty as they were off on holiday themselves the next day, and wouldn't be getting their bulk meat order delivered until their return. "Here's the key, feel free".

So we trundled the wheelbarrow many times up and down the road to their garage on what felt like the hottest day of the year, laden with rapidly frosting boxes of raspberries and currants, bulging bags of gooseberries, let alone the lasagne and microchips! In a week we had our splendid new chest freezer delivered and reversed the procedure, more than a little grateful to good friends and kind neighbours, nothing wasted, nothing lost.

Monday
James asked me to do a trim on one of our houseplants. Unfortunately I trimmed in error (and innocence), the wrong one, so now we have an abbreviated lemon as well as orange tree! Poor communication.

Pruned (correctly this time) the buddleias at each end of the plots. We like the newer one that Brian gave us, a Dorset cutting. It has grown so quickly and in its first year produced its delightful stubby chrome-yellow flowerheads. James leaves the pruning until nearly March and then cuts them down pretty fiercely and it seems to work. You get less woody growth building up and they make up their height in the summer months quite amazingly.

Finishing up days now, last onions, parsnips, but the shallots are still useable with only a few going soft on me.

March

USUAL Tai Chi evening class. Talked to Harry in the break and learned that many years ago he used to have a plot on our site, in fact it was the renowned Rocky's plot! The old boy had been a bit pinchpenny (he said), and scorned proper supports for his raspberries using cut twigs and branches instead. Harry found himself inheriting a positive coppice of rooted twigs! He thinks that the monument near the park is definitely a horse's grave . . . I didn't argue . . . James says "dog"; but who knows . . . small horse, big dog!

Wednesday
Stewed some fresh rhubarb for supper. How it diminishes almost as bad as spinach. Had given some to Meg next door as she loves it, Mike doesn't so she seldom buys it in the shops so it comes as a treat for her.

Heard a topical tip on the radio . . . "Dig

up all your leek plants now and heel them in until wanted". This lets you get on with preparing the ground for new season things. Also they said get your really early "earlies" in now, this the fourteenth of March.

Sunday
Glorious day, both overdid things with Spring-like enthusiasm, not wanting to stop.

Alf was seeing in some new plot-holders, a middle-aged couple with a bored daughter, remote with her headset, disinterested in rods and soil structure, a reluctant third of the trio.

Ruth's Jack Russell was on site today unfortunately, its scampering and yapping a noisy nuisance. When the foxes are around it goes quite mad and choking barking noises mark their jousting spot. James teases her saying that the fox will undoubtedly "win" and will she get another Jack Russell?

Actually we very much doubt if the fox would win an outright battle proper as they seem less aggressive in fact and maybe have a less vicious nip. Usually there is no victor after these affrays and JR is hauled away, protesting, by Ruth to be banished to her car until she is ready to go home. Imprisoned, he barks non-stop! I suppose dogs don't know that plots have boundaries and can be forgiven but not their owners. Alf says he must get a reminder up about the part of our lease that stipulates "dogs to be kept on leashes at all times". The foxes set an example with their narrow light feet, picking their chosen route, delicately, across the allotments seldom causing much damage unless choosing to scrape or burrow under some precious crop!

★ ★ ★

Christopher Robin has had the Tunisian 'flu and the benefits of her holiday seem to have been obliterated by nasty symptoms. She sits on her little stool using her long-handled small fork to do a bit of weeding but is lethargic. We discuss our dahlias, her snow-white one, our pink one and finalise our swap. James always digs the tubers up and stores them in the greenhouse in the winter but she leaves hers in and they seem to survive. However, it will be an easier job for James to break off some dry sprouting tubers than to divide cleanly her earthbound plants. We'll see anyway when the time comes.

Picked some chard leaves, it is getting a bit stumpy now but still edible. Picked some of the early polyanthus flowerheads for pressing . . . orange, bright magenta, cream, but sadly I put the polythene bag in the fridge and forgot them so all were wasted.

Thursday
Put in the onion sets and covered with a net to prevent the birds tweaking them out. Think they use the dry bits for nesting material. Still eating the tail end of last year's crop but most of these are splitting now and shooting.

The Desirees are sprouting too. I lifted the lid of the potato crock and saw masses of pale stems rearing up at me. All the little spuds were sprouting like mad in their dark container. I don't mind "heralds of Spring" but these seemed to be making a positive protest! However, I broke them off and boiled the potatoes proper in their skins for a soup base.

Evenings are getting better now, soon will be able to go up to the plot after tea. Last week bought courgette, parsley and tarragon seeds.

Friday
Watched two parakeets flying around the plot, squarking . . . survivors from the severe winter. Hoping the tribe will build up again to the previous five or six, feeding in our garden at the top of our nut-pole. (Left-over tubes from the children's garden Badminton set).

It seemed to be years before James finally devised a squirrel proof barrier efficient enough to prevent them from nipping up the pole to steal the nuts. We used to watch amazed at the efforts they made to reach the food, leaping from bending fragile branches a great distance away, slithering down the greased pole but persevering! Now we have an inverted, large plastic flower pot suspended a foot or so underneath, which seems to work. It had to be big and rather unsightly as a smaller version was soon mastered by the squirrels, making it stable against the pole and then levering themselves up and over. This one defeats them and they sit on the fence or on the shed, tail twitching, baffled at last. The nut bell too remains a no-go area for them as this is suspended on the finest twig to take its full weight, and any squirrel attempting plunder will pitch off although I am sure that one day even this will be solved by one brighter, lighter creature.

At home, out of the kitchen window I look onto one of the left over cabbage plants. (James never throws any growing thing away!). The great flourishing head of green is battling with the azalea bush beside it and swamping my forget-me-nots. By the time it has hearted up if it ever does, I expect the shrubs will be in full bloom. Looking forward to the doronicums flowering now, bright yellow daisy-heads in their square patch of green. Very welcome and nicer than daffs in a way as they don't collapse in the Spring winds. Last year we had terrible hail storms and all the broad leafed plants had great puncture holes scarring them the whole summer through.

Saturday
Percy has given us five autumn fruiting raspberry plants which we plan to put in replacing the Himalayan Giant blackberry. This was advertised as being so fruitful that you could pick "a bucketful of berries weekly in season". Not entirely true we found out when we planted our purchase by the fence in our garden. A vigourous grower, yes, but not quite that amount of fruit! After a couple of years we moved it up to the plot where it flourished entangling the raspberries and our clothes gleefully every summer, yielding moderate crops. So it has been banished to the park chainlink fence now, the newish stretch the park-people put up after the gale damage. It romps along now, unrestrained and duly supplying "bucketfuls" to any brave picker who doesn't mind getting scratched and torn in the process.

The hellebore flowers are quite beautiful, mauve, green and spotted cream, they seem bursting with good health and obviously love their spot by the park under the sycamore and beeches.

Sunday
Dug leeks, picked spinach and found a few sprouts still. The pigeons are making a feast of the uncovered broccoli. The onions are sprouting but need weeding. The next door but one plotholder has finally dug over part of his plot and planted a row of polyanthus along the path edge, he has also put in three pillar roses. He has either turned over a very new leaf or the plot has changed hands!

★ ★ ★

Did some home hoeing while James sowed seeds in peat pots. Must look out all those little envelopes of kept seeds- wild "sweet pea"; Sally's calendula; orange pansies from Bexhill and columbine from Leeds. I often forget to do this each year or have not labelled and dated them, so end up having to throw them away as they are either unidentifiable or stale by then! Failed with poppies last year as all the hoped-for doubles turned out as dreary little singles which seeded themselves everywhere.

Good Friday
Very, very cold wind. After church changed into warmer things, woolly hats and scarves, socks and wellies. My left one is split so put a plastic bag over my sock first, it hadn't rained recently so this should do. James couldn't find his gloves so lent him mine which are in fact his own old cast-off driving ones, all dried up and brittle now from much use but good for keeping out the prickles. I had to wear beige knitted ones, they'll be a proper mess.

Really horrid chilly wind cutting right through everything. Wish I had put on long-johns. You can hear the trains clearly as if they were careering across the allotments. The aeroplane noise comes in gusts too. There are quite a few people working, Terry has evidently had a few days off from work, so that's why his plot looks so different! The roses aren't pillar he says, but standards on briars. He says his father used to "breed" tea roses this way and he is going to have a go.

We uncover the onion sets so that they can be hoed. There are masses of weeds mostly chickweed and bindweed, plus sycamore seedlings. It is too muddy to do much good though as the soil is sticky and heavy. I wear my glasses so that I can see the onion tips but my eyes still water with the cold and I have to keep blowing off the nose drips as I can't be bothered to fish for a tissue with muddy gloves. The drops sail away horizontally in the fierce wind!

The rhubarb is well up. The newer crowns put in last year (and left unpicked as instructed in spite of temptation) are higher than the older ones we moved, but all look healthy. The old stock in the freezer is still quite considerable so must start to use it up for chutney or whatever, soon.

Tuesday pm
Up to Fulham for lunch. Took a collection of things from the plot, "My lovely Harvest Festival!" says Aunt Alice, ever appreciative. We had to confess that

it was last season's mint and gooseberry jelly and that a speck of mould had been removed but this was no worry. She showed us the planted mint we had given her, potted last year and thriving on her balcony. She has quite a garden out there in spite of its size, and a bird sanctuary too. In the spring the air is sweet with the scent of hyacinths, later the geraniums and pelagoniums flourish and the birds leave their grateful mark on the leaves. Every patch of wall is used and she achieves her own mini crop of runner beans each summer. Today it is our frozen ones we eat for lunch, enjoying a shared meal in her kitchen.

Toby the cat excels himself with batting at a bluebottle and finally eating it and then spends the afternoon glaring at a blue tit on the nut feeder. In fact he is a very nice cat and has brought down Aunt Alice's blood pressure she says, so is forgiven. In the cold weather he lies along the top of the pretend 'coal' fire and so far has not singed his tail on the elements, pulling it up in his sleep just in time as it slowly sinks down towards the heat.

We told her about the pretty blue nuthatch we had seen in our garden and what was going on up at the allotments. She is particularly interested in our site as when a young girl, she had lived close by for many years. Then it was "the big house" inhabited by a well-heeled local family. She knew them quite well and remembers one high summer when the boys camped out on the lawn. However this gentle safari was supervised by their mother, most particular, and she had insisted that each boy should have his own potty under his camp bed duly collected and emptied by the appropriately named chamber maid each morning!

She remembers the house and lovely gardens well and there were even cows in a field nearby then.

My own earliest recollections are of a big sad looking house and great aircraft guns in the forecourt and grounds, providing a defence, we hoped, in the Blitz; a lot of noise and shrapnel amongst the crisscross of searchlights and barrage balloons, . . . noisier times.

Now our site is peaceful and productive.

We still have the shed at the top end where the mowers are housed, stores of fertilisers, chairs for a rest.

Down our end we have a long, low building which was part of the stable block. At one end it is "Ladies Only" kept private by a wooden door secured with a twig through a metal ring. Once inside you just have to whistle. The interior is a miniature room with rugs on the uneven stone floor, a dressing table with flyblown mirror, faded orange runner with fringed ends, a small bedroom chair and of course the essential chemical closet. An ancient but still relevant notice reads — "pennies only please or the kind plotholder may not wish to continue her job in changing this!", this in the handwriting of the dear departed lady Hon. Sec . . . The toilet roll holder remains empty and the plot "ladies" wisely bring their own tissues or the like. For us though it is a refuge, allows us to remain like Winnie, for long hours on the site. It has its own quaint if aromatic charm. The "gents" is further along the building, less gracious I am told being a gulley where we imagine the water ran when the horses' stalls were being mucked out, but it serves.

Were able to identify a plant from Aunt Alice's new flower book as a Dracunculus Vulgaris, near tropical. It came, like our hydrangea from Minna's cottage garden but she had always called it "Mephistopheles"! It is a good name as it rears up on its blotched stem, pretty evil, as the great purple flower has a revolting-smelling spike which attracts blowflies which pollinate the thing. The stem is attractive though and the early spring foliage welcome and bright. We had always hoped that the fertilised spike would turn to a display of berries as in Lords and Ladies, a relative, but we have never achieved anything, only a depleted drooping spike and the relief that it no longer pretends to be rotting carrion!

We left Aunt Alice leaning over her balcony to see us off. We wave goodbye to each other until we are out of sight and the car has turned the corner.

Friday
Quick visit to dig up leeks and parsnips for the weekend. Neighbours were tying

up their new raspberry canes and having a bonfire. A lot of digging has been done around us. You can tell which plots belong to the retired ones who are always well ahead with more time to spare "up the plot"! Most of the planted garlic are well and truly up, seven green spikes so far, and the covered broad beans doing fine.

Finished edges started two weeks earlier but they will need a proper "slicing" with James' new sharp spade to make it really neat and deep.

James has finished digging the last patch ready for onion sets which are beginning to sprout back home on a tray in the garden room.

Picked two new angelica leaves, (plants now recovered from the February frosts) to put in with the rhubarb for lunch, takes away that odd dry sensation in your mouth. I imagine it would do the same for spinach.

Sunday
Gooseberry bushes now showing a bit of colour. Covered them with loose netting hopefully this will stop the wretched

finches "nipping them in the bud".

Saw the Hon. Sec. and discussed the possibility of doing a Summer painting course up the allotments, in June.

★ ★ ★

Discovered more of Rose's self sown little angelica plants thriving among the weeds, can't ever see us making her recipe for a heady, convent-originated liqueur. James poorly so no sowing today as planned. Went up alone with the trolley and fork to do a bit of harvesting for the week. Sunday pm is usually quiet, no cars in the car park. Disturbed a fat wood pigeon demolishing some golden crocuses, what messy creatures they are! Saw a bee in a patch of the stubbier creamy ones, not on our plot but near the shed.

Tuesday
Birdsong stronger. Changed shoes as it is still very muddy and forked up some parsnips. Not much foliage left now but worked along what was left of the two rows. (Should be sowing more today).

Not bad state with clean roots and only a few forked ones. Dug up four leeks. They seem to have stuck at one size and not fattened up much this season. Lastly, pulled up six stems of the finished brussels, stripped them ready for burning and cleaned and stacked the canes that had been supporting them since quite small, all their long life in fact. This seems to work keeping them straight and wind resistant. Have been harvesting since last October, goodness knows how many pounds!

Mrs Somme was up there too. Tells me that she intends to fill her new bit of plot with soft fruits. She also wants to get rid of the pussy willow tree which the oriental gentleman had put in before she took over. I don't see why not, it is attractive but not edible. Fruit trees are allowed, and flowers up to one third I believe is the site guide, but hardly willows? She said I could take some branches and as I had my secateurs was able to gather some. I thought, as I clipped cleanly, of childhood's memory, of Spring country walks, the tantalising tough stems of silky buds, finding that you twisted and tugged in vain to break off a twig or two, and having, ashamedly, to leave behind a messy bit of half-parted twig. My fingers are stronger now but less likely to pick anything that grows wild, better understanding the need for conservation.

Saturday
Lovely bare brown soil nearly all dug over . . . I admire, James digs!

He is sowing more broad beans now as the November lot never came to anything much. He does not think that it was the weather this time expecting typical frostbitten shoots but maybe it was the greedy black crows, there seem to be a lot of these monsters around now, even more than wood pigeons. Great stabbing beaks, horrid creatures!

Sunday am
Very chilly wind today. On Saturday had sown some onion sets, and two rows of parsnips. Had a bonfire which went up like a rocket with all the dried raspberry canes. Spent a couple of cold hours working and looked forward to returning

to a chicken and jacket potatoes. The rhubarb looks red and healthy, the two newer crowns more advanced than the older ones. Seems the wrong way round but maybe it is a different kind.

James dug in the soft rubbish from the sprouts where he was preparing the potato beds. We noticed that some of the roots waiting to be burned still had the original peat pots on them. Because of the dreaded club root he always sows them in clean soil in pots which seems to work. Borrowed Mrs Somme's "swoe" from the shed as we had forgotten to bring our own two hoes and cleaned up between the leek rows also around the gooseberries. Hope our non-pruning year will not affect the crop too adversely.

Overheard some tart comments about Mrs Somme's plot and we defended its somewhat zany appearance. She is a little eccentric maybe and it is certainly visually patchy to say the least (hence our naming of the owner affectionately . . . "Mrs. Somme"). There are countless metal frames, bits of polythene, inverted jam and sweet jars, tights tieing up frail stems (efficiently) and piles of plastic water bottles lie waiting for her watering sessions, sensibly carried out by loading one of the wheelbarrows with a stack of filled manageable containers. All very practical but apparently not seemly enough for the more particular plotholders. "People will always help harvest fruit" says Mrs Somme, quite rightly and in goes another currant bush.

Tuesday am
James dug a bit more of the top plot saying that if it looked half complete by next time, it would seem less of a burden, true, but the keen wind drove us home before he could get that far.

Phil walked down for a chat and bonemeal was mentioned. She made us laugh by saying that Daisy would always bark at the bag of bonemeal in the garden shed and wondered what she was trying to say!

Frank phoned later in the day to say that he had sold our order of seed potatoes to someone else by mistake. We should have picked them up this morning but forgot . . . must be the cold.

Shall have more time soon when the clocks go forward (leaping into Spring!) and the days get longer. We can pop up for a bit of work before dark. There is still a little digging left to do and some lettuces to sow under cloches.

Friday
The rescued sweet pea seedlings in the greenhouse look fit, three or four inches high. Father used to use our plot to have his own row of these when we first had an allotment. In fact it was his idea that we should become plotholders in the first place. The allotments were nearer his house than ours in fact and all the neighbours were offered associate membership of the site. He encouraged us to join as full members and asked if he might have a small area on which to grow his beloved sweet peas, his garden "not being suitable" he said. Of course we agreed. As he had been forbidden to smoke we were amused to notice his frequent visits to see how his plants were getting on and the little puffs of smoke seen but not referred to or given away.

41

But his deception was our gain as it was the start of an unending enthusiasm for being plotholders. Nor did the occasional puff seem to do him any noticeable harm.

Saturday
Did a thorough weed all around the herbs and took a rest sitting on the pile of kerbstones by the shed. A bit chilly on the bum but a nice height for a short-legged individual! What we need is a sturdy wooden seat down the car park end, (the posh end of the site have one of course, facing a green sward of carefully tended grass!). Maybe we could have just a piece of warmer wood as a "bench"? The worry is that a decent one might get stolen as we are more accessible to the road and park our end, it might "do a walk" as James says. This particular corner has been cleared quite recently and people with spare plants and shrubs bring them along for Alf to vet. Gradually the spot has become civilised with montbretia, azaleas, berberis thriving in the ancient leafy soil and there is plenty of space for annuals in the summertime,

(not forgetting the energetic Himalayan Giant!)

Pride of place is given to a Crimson King tree, this was our donation. James was having nightmares about roots and subsidence at home even though the tree was quite a distance from the house. We had bought it to replace a selfsown (I thought magnificent) Ash and then realised that our new tree would probably be far too big, a silly choice but we loved the colour. Alf said he would be delighted to give it a home in the new area by the car park so when it was a suitable time he came down with the van and he and James dug it up with as much soil and root ball as they could manage. Earlier, James had done a good job preparing the hole where the tree was to be planted, digging deep and filling it with lots of rich welcoming compost but he could not go with Alf and the tree that day, having something else to attend to.

"Missing the tree-planting ceremony? Shame!" says Alf having a roll-up before setting off for the allotments.

He arrives at the site and starts to unload the tree asking a plotholder if he could give him a hand.

"Planting the tree for James" he grunts as they heave it down from the van-top.

"Oh dear" says the helper, "I didn't know he had died!" . . . !

Monday
Met Ruth at the greengrocers on the corner just as they were putting their outside display away. She needed some fresh coriander but seemed a little unsure what she was asking for! She hadn't seemed the type to be over fussy culinary-wise but you never can tell.

"You should be growing it yourself" I teased.

"Oh no" the Italian greengrocer said, "No, no, far too cold here!" giving me my broccoli and a squeeze of the arm at the same time.

She got her own back as we walked down the road together, seeing my bunch of bananas sticking out of the basket, "Don't you grow your own?" but all this in good humour.

April

Wednesday

DIGGING, planting, sowing. French beans, lettuce and lettuce plants under cloches. Leeks, beetroots, spinach, tomato seeds in the greenhouse, and runner beans too.

Sunday

James is trying something new but related to Mrs Somme's rubbish sacks, that is, warming the soil. We have bought a new sheet of polythene and spread it all over the area where the corn plants are to go. He has secured all the edges with a layer of earth so it should stay in place unless the fox gets curious and does an exploratory dig. We noticed an old metal cold frame lying near the shed and wondered if it was going "free". First, we commandeered it, taking it up to our top end by the box, then had second thoughts, a bit of conscience, and put it back where it came from! It was just the frame with a hinged lid squarely fixed, in working order, and a single pane of glass. As it turns out, Alf tells us that it was actually left for Miss Tear, (one of our recent human acquisitions). She and her housekeeper-cum-friend, Miriam, are making great inroads on a plot that was originally not only dull but a disaster, with a fly-by-night owner who soon lost heart after a couple of setbacks and a disapproving spouse. He survived his first year and then gave up. The trouble is, as Alf says, is that "people" give up and don't tell him and their plots get shaggier and shaggier until someone realises that the tenant has gone missing for good. This makes the job of clearing the patch for another person much more difficult obviously.

When James left the site and was shutting the gates he saw a great tit enter a hole at the foot of the street lamp — an inspection trap used for maintenance probably. Maybe it is nesting there? Had seen Robby kneeling down there Mecca-wise earlier in the week, thought "funny . . . !", expect he was curious too.

Saw a fox the other evening trotting into the car park area with a bird in its mouth, he kept to the path and disappeared into the park. Digging the FINAL patch . . . disturbed a frog. Robins and thrushes now permanent company.

The park trees are still etched and fine against grey skies. There are fat buds on the elderberry trees but no silver and gold now that Mrs Somme has taken out the pussy willow. A few daffs are out on the higher plots but we don't go in for flowers much, finding the vegetables and herbs sufficiently decorative. The slim irises near the car park end are an exception and gradually little patches of perennials are appearing where we give homes to plants in need of fostering from overcrowded gardens, ours included.

Saw three blackbirds foraging together amicably, two male one female not bothered about territorial rights it seemed, room for all up there.

Friday
Mrs Somme's bits of black plastic covering her battlefield are in danger of taking off in the Spring winds. Our

five full bags of corporation leaves will need emptying soon, probably put them into the runner bean trench. I suspect that when we lift them up we will find a whole patch of pale mint shoots just waiting to take over the water tank corner! Today's mint jelly with our lamb joint comes from this source, the variety with soft greyish-green leaves, I think it is apple mint. Sometimes I sneak some from the next plot, we share the path anyway, and mix these in too. His plants have glossier, narrow leaves and the taste is different, sharper. I have taken a piece of root home and put it in a tub so that I'll have a kitchen supply but must not let it take over the herbaceous border.

The children had a lovely pungent mint in their Canadian garden in Calgary. I took a tiny piece with a fragment of root on it and tucked it in my makeup purse when we returned to the UK after our holiday there. It didn't seem to mind the flight, all those tedious miles in the sky and now flourishes in a terracotta pot among the other kinds, sitting right under the overflow hole of the top water tank.

It has a much smaller leaf and a reddish stem.

Saturday am
Ought to start cleaning up the strawberry beds. Chilly wind but absolutely clear pale skies. There are patches of warmth in the house where the sun strikes the carpet or chair, like those sudden welcome sea patches when swimming in shallow waters. On the plot though the wind is keen everywhere but we soon get really warm inside our thick coats and start to shed woolly hats and scarves pretty soon. The strawberry bed is muddly with much ground elder flourishing and we wonder if we should leave it alone for now and sort it all after the fruiting season. Better still we decide, to abandon these plants and buy fresh ones, using a different part of the plot altogether for the new bed.

Parsnips still not up, after four weeks! Maybe we should sow some more! We have done this before also with carrots, only to find that we were overly impatient and had a mixed double row difficult to thin.

James has had a word with Miss Tear

and all is well. We are to share the cold frame and he is to repair it! Fair enough, but it may be some time before he gets around to it, there always seems so much to do. However, it is back by the box again and no doubt, one fine day, will be made as good as new when taken off the bottom of our list of "things to do".

Monday
Trotting up the path with his Marks and Spencers carrier bag comes the bee keeper with a huge pickle jar full of syrup for his hive. He tells us that this cold spell is bad for them as they are "working" now and could starve. His hive was vandalised last summer by some idiots who cut through the park fence and tipped it over. Only some bees survived and then only because he came up in the night with a torch, I suppose when someone had told him of the trouble, and "put them together again". He is wearing his white overalls and heavy gloves and we can see him at work through the trees up by the compost heap. I asked him the other day why my friend had been attacked repeatedly

50

by some bees the other side of her garden fence when she was quite quietly doing some gardening. He said that it might be because they were queenless, evidently they become irritable and idle without a leader — We had wondered if it was hair spray or some other matter they took offence to. We remembered the woman plotholder who came shrieking and tearing at her hair once, hurtling down the allotment path. She ended up dunking her head in the water tank which seemed to have the right effect albeit a bit drastic! In fact apart from this one instance, none of us have come to any harm from the allotment hives and are glad to see the bees enjoying the hyssop flowers and angelica heads, fertilising the soft fruits and vegetables for us.

Some of the hives are up by the old monument. We asked Aunt Alice if she remembered it, what secret burial it enshrined, as the plaque has gone. Was it for a favourite pet, a dog, a pony perhaps? Like Harry, she did not know, could only guess. It used to have an iron railing all around it but now there are only a few bent spikes left and broken supports. We have looked for any sign of an inscription but there is none, only a carved swathe and laurel wreath.

When we tried to clear some of the devastation of the Great Storm we uncovered traces of the foxes entrance and exit areas, flattened by their to-ings and fro-ings near the monument. Lords and ladies flourish there, some with leaves spotted with black, others plain green, a relative of our Mephistopheles as we know now. The name "Lords and Ladies" is explained in two ways by our flower books. One says that the mauve or white flowers look like elegant courtiers, the other seems more acceptable as it suggests that the name comes from the fact that the plant was used to make a kind of starch for the ruffs in Tudor times. Sometimes plant names are a bit on the ribald side to say the least but these seem quite respectable and sedate. The plot can bring out the naughty side of you and I always get the giggles when harvesting those fine upstanding broad bean pods, (broad beans contain aphrodisiac properties we understand, as well as being highly suggestive visually!), and James has been known to dangle the odd courgette, ("boasting again!")

The couple who used to rent our newer plot were usually diligent workers but occasionally disappeared behind the untamed undergrowth up by the park, for their "lunch". We never disturbed them and they left their black and white collie to guard their gardening tools! They did work hard though and we were sorry to see them go. Evidently they looked after an old people's home and the owners did a runner, so suddenly, no job and they had to leave to look for employment elsewhere. We waited awhile, then as no one took over the plot relieved it of their three new soft fruit bushes which transferred well.

Tuesday pm
Runner beans — Soaked them, those that floated to the top threw away. Left the others in the water until they were as wrinkled as a "washerwoman's". This was the midwife's description of baby Sarah's hands. Newborn, ten days overdue, her tiny pink fingers were very wrinkly, "Too long in your water" reassured the midwife

and in a little while they became perfect, like the rest of her.

The trench awaiting the plants later is being filled regularly with leaves, well rotted, tops of vegetables, old vests, anything that will rot down well. James hedges his bets putting some beans in pots and others directly into the ground. If it is a cold Spring then the seeds sown outside are slower to appear obviously but catch up in the end. Any gaps can be filled with the ones raised in the greenhouse, (half soil, half peat) and a bit of double booking does no harm.

Helped James put in short sticks to act as supports for the broad bean plants, we then take string along so that they have this too to prevent them from collapsing or getting blown down. We fasten the strings carefully so that we can slide them up keeping up with the growing plants as they get taller.

Hooray, the parsnips are up at last!

James dug up some of the biggest leeks and thinking I was being helpful, I trimmed off their tops only to find out that he had marked these out for a still life arrangement for the art class, wanting ALL the bits and pieces! Never mind, there were plenty more for "art".

We can still see Saint Edmund's; Christ Church; the Congregational now called United Reform; but the foliage buds on the trees surrounding the site are fattening up now and are already screening the Parish and Saint Barnabas which are to be heard but not seen now.

Part of our old climbing frame metal rods have appeared on the next plot so rescued them as they make useful props. We leave the basic metal poles for the runners in all the year and then add canes for the actual climbing season. You are supposed to move the crop, for rotation, but it is less trouble this way and we compensate with the regular trenching and feeding, it seems to work anyway.

Sunday am
Timed it badly this weekend as it was a splendid day yesterday but much rain in the early hours and all the morning today, so spent some time in the greenhouse potting things. Had to get some broccoli so drove up to a deserted plot, except for

a tailless blackbird and one squirrel. The broccoli is doing well in spite of the early attacks by those wretched pigeons and we picked a basketful. Cut some spinach too and will do a pancake dish for tonight.

It has been a showery week with some really heavy rain. The soil is sticky black, too tacky for sowing and impossible to hoe. What we really need is a couple of fine dry days, a bit of a breeze and then we can get going with the radish and lettuce — it will all "catch up" anyway. Identified a bit of puzzling birdsong today. It is a great tit. He was up in the park beech trees but this time, could be seen and identified properly. Our robin came really close as we planted four rows of maincrop Desiree potatoes. James gave me a measured stick so that I could put them in evenly spaced, ever particular!

Thursday
Plenty of broccoli to pick, I like their cut-and-come again character, much better than once-off cauliflowers. The pigeons are being kept off by our netting it seems, but one leaf, straggling outside had been

pecked to a mere skeleton which shows how necessary our precautions are. The perpetual spinach gave us another good picking and half an hour later we were eating it, stalks and all! We get quite smug and nutritious minded when we do this, feeling that there must be great benefit to our systems with such unparalleled freshness. We are in danger of being "freshness bores" maybe.

Broad beans in good flower, need some nice warm sunshine and bees to pollinate them. I wonder how the hives are? The plotholders prone to flower crops are displaying red tulips galore and there are still some daffs and narcissi around. People with polyanthus wisely cover the blooms with cottons or netting. Noticed some blossom on the currant bushes, delicate dark pink tiny flowers.

Onion sets look much better, about five inches of green showing. Parsnips all right but a bit choked with chickweed. It is still too sticky to weed around the seedlings.

The leeks can be pulled up by hand quite cleanly as the soil is so wet. "Hold them firmly though or they'll snap" I am told. I concentrate as I pull, thinking of the roots down below and can hear the snapping and squeaking as they draw up. They are dirty and full of mud where the leaves crisscross, holding yesterday's showers, a messy affair but you soon learn to shake off the soil with care or you get a stream of cold water up your sleeve!

The horse chestnut trees in the park are becoming more Spring-like with down-turned hands of green fingers. Hear our first woodpecker today. Looking forward to the swifts returning to St. Barnabas's eaves, the first sign of real "summer".

Saturday pm
The geese in the park were very honky today, but the sound was not as irritating as the peacock noises we had to bear last year. The birds were donated by a wellwisher but it all went wrong. The two hens and two cockbirds were put in a pen under the giant cedar tree on one of the lawns near the lake. Somehow they kept on escaping, ending up on the posh houses' rooftops . . . (do they fly? they must obviously). Anyway,

the householders became thoroughly fed up with this unsolicited "gift" to the Borough, with these birds invading their property and emitting their doleful and eerie cries, day and night. They were transferred in disgrace to a private residence and never seen again. The park returned to its usual clamour of waterbirds, geese and ducks who know their place.

There seem to be more seagulls in the park than ever. You cannot really call them "sea" gulls for I am sure that they have never seen the sea and they certainly never give that typical lilting seaside cry, only squawk. When we arrive on a family visit to Broadstairs the first sound we hear is that lovely call. These park cousins are very urban, taking part in games of bread throwing and catching, vieing with the ducks, enjoying the stale bread not meant for them. (Children enjoy it too. I can recall the taste of duck's-bread crusts, old, buttery and hard! Now I watch the grandchildren consume the same fare, in the same park). The gulls seem to have an information team so that as soon as you put out meaty scraps in the back garden they appear from nowhere, to fight it out with starlings and pigeons, a mass of thrashing greedy wings.

Saw four jays this week hopping about in the cherry tree where the buds are just about to explode. It only takes a day to change from buds to a great haze of blossom. In a while the parakeets come and peck at the flowers. They seem to know how pretty they look, bright green against white, and cock their heads looking at us, looking at them. Do they eat the nectary blossom or is it just mild vandalism? Anyway they make a regular confetti of chopped flowers at the foot of the tree.

Tuesday
In the evening sowed radishes down the middle of the bean trenches. Noticed that some of the runners were poking through, hope they won't be "topped" by a late frost. Sowed lettuce seed by the gooseberry bushes, already covered in tiny set fruit. Raised the support strings for the broad beans, lots of flowers.

Dug out some more ground elder

from the path and James thinks he is really winning now on the top plot. Mrs Somme has put piles of weeds in the hollow of the main path, our M1, but maybe squashed down with a bit of soil this will help to build it up. Everyone uses our two side paths and they get really worn down to a single hollow track from all those trundled wheelbarrows.

★ ★ ★

Must remember to net the gooseberry bushes soon.

Saturday
Freak hot spell, amazing sunshine, in the seventies! The man with the two noisy little boys was very much in evidence over the weekend, stripped to the waist and bright burned pink over his stooped back and shoulders. The boys quarrelled and whined and got in the way. Alf fears that he will have to give one of his warnings soon as the plot rarely gets any attention at all, and the few sporadic bursts are not really enough to keep things under control. He makes

allowances but has to draw the line eventually.

We were scorched too as we both got down to grub up the weeds set fast among the raspberries. Up the new plot it was much cooler and we spent a little time there lying on our "nearly-lawn" area by the Hellebores. The Acuba suckers from home seem to have taken and gradually it is becoming less of a wilderness.

Great birdsong everywhere and a yaffle in full laugh. The blue speedwell is as bright as the row of forget-me-nots we planted along the path edge by the upper tank. These originated from self-sown ones and have proved a very useful demarcation of where our new plot finishes and the wild bit by the site compost heap begins. The cow parsley seems to have grown a foot in a week.

As we weed, two silly boys in the park keep calling out, mainly to annoy Mrs Somme who, like us, is working hard in the sunshine. "Hello Grandma" they keep on calling, giggling, repeating, more irritating than really rude. We all manage to ignore them as they clamber over the remnants of the fallen beech the other side of the link fence. Expect their respective families will be glad when school starts again and the holiday, for the kids, is over. Later in the day three little girls follow, the same park route but had no interest in us. They picked their cautious way over the tree delicately, talking quietly to each other, half-heard by us . . . sugar and spice!

★ ★ ★

Mrs Somme bemoaned the curiosity of the foxes and showed us where one had torn one of her plastic sheets, disturbing the covered soil beneath in spite of two heavy stakes pushed through to secure it. There were big dug-out holes, "wretched nuisances" she grumbles as she fills in the foxy holes and footprints. She discovers a single man's shoe and we are puzzled too as to its origin . . . a one-legged plotholder? We accept her kind offer of some spinach.

Divided the clump of lovage as it has grown too big and put by a piece for Terry as promised.

Learn that our Chairman of the Allotment Society is over ninety years old and wonder if he will make this year's annual show, presiding on the platform as usual.

Were both glad to get home and have a good wash. The strong salt taste as I had licked my lips had surprised me as we grubbed away among the raspberry canes. Not an April taste somehow, smacking more of high summer. As we had worked layers of clothes had come off, buttons undone with the T-shirt doing the final mopping of the sweat, all very earthy!

A raspberry cane had scratched my forearm quite badly and I had tasted more salt as I licked off the trail of blood.

Friday pm
Terribly heavy showers today, thunder and lightning, wind and rain, then bright warm sunshine and clear skies — shilly-shallying weather!

Woodpecker drilling away somewhere; lots of noisy birdsong and a hysterical blackbird on the beanpoles.

Plenty of aircraft but not Concorde

today. The usual flight paths busy but most planes hidden by big bruised cloud formations.

★ ★ ★

Saw first bluebell in flower by the park fence. Picked early rhubarb, really good thick stems. The rhubarb leaves have great pierced holes in them from hailstones, they look more like cheese-plants. Noticed our breath was smoking so must still be quite chilly.

How things change weatherwise from day to day!

Mrs Somme's battlefield looks quite authentic this evening. The storms have knocked down some of the plastic and wooden contraptions and tossed bits all over the place, there is authentic mud in her trenches too.

Monday pm

Very heavy showers again. The car park was really boggy and there were smooth lines of mud where it had silted down. Our lower plot becomes flooded easily with a sudden downpour as the slope brings it all down to our end.

Once we lost a whole crop of stuff there when it was completely flooded but there is the usual compensation, for when damp conditions are needed and everything else is parched, some things flourish. Like our iris, and the marrows! Saw one very early strawberry flower right out already on Terry's plot.

Thursday

Mrs Somme was confronted by James today complaining about a great pile of ground elder and assorted weeds on a black plastic sheet on our top plot. Orderly in theory but not there when we are trying hard to knock it into shape.

"My method" she tells him disregarding where they lie . . . "but not mine" replies James unusually curt. Later they both apologise and all is amiable again.

However, he is right when he guesses that if we are not careful to make this plot look cared for, we shall have it used, as before, as a short cut to the site compost heap area and traversed by all and sundry. My original idea for a grassy strip running parallel to the two apple trees is not a good one I now agree and we shall plant rows of beetroots on the one side, brussels on the other.

Christopher Robin has found her gloves, it seems that she had put them down in her garage somewhere so all is well. She is so-named by us (affectionately) because of her regular allotment Spring to Autumn "uniform"; this comprises floppy white cotton hat, short-sleeved shirt or T-shirt, short shorts and high black wellies. Her whole boyish figure calls to mind a Shepherd drawing even though she must be five times his subject's age. She usually brings with her an old rush-seated stool on which she takes a well-earned rest from her labours or uses it to get her on the right level for attacking the buttercups and ground elder.

She has taken over the plot from her rather taciturn son who has left the district and a legacy for her of underdug ground and many weeds. We must ask Alf what her real name is as it seems awkward now, after all this time of casual neighbourly acquaintance . . . British reticence!

Her helper arrived midday last Saturday, more talking than digging done as usual, their voices carried on the light breeze, with much leaning on forks and contemplating. "He does it for kindness, not cash" she tells us and we suspect that the sharing of the labour and the company is as helpful to her as the rather spasmodic turning of the soil.

Wednesday

Alf has had a hernia operation. He called in at home for a cup of tea and a grumble about the hospital. It seems that he was all prepped up for the op' and then sent home! The next morning he goes in as instructed and waits for ages but no one comes to give him his pre-med' but the two jolly porters arriving to "take him down" say, "never mind" and trundle him off to the anaesthetic bay, stone cold sober!

The room smells of his diminutive roll-ups long after he has gone but we have been well entertained as usual, and pleased to see him well and reasonably sound.

Later in the day we go up to the plot and find Miriam there, working away. She would like another piece of plot but Miss Tear, knowing the temptations of Miriam re gardening, has put her foot down and told her "No". However, Miss Tear goes off quite frequently to foreign parts in pursuit of interesting birds so Miriam has a field-day while her employer follows the cranes . . . USA; Russia: the world seems to be hers!

The apple blossom is out and the plum too and so far it looks as if the fruits will set. The angelica plants are over six feet high and seem to be earlier this year. The hellebore flowers continue to delight us and others, with their great sprays of flowers and bright foliage.

James has sown his corn seeds in pots like toilet roll centres, guaranteed "biodegradable"?

I have at long last attended to the plastic seed tray of nicotianas and pricked out a mere 180 mini-plants!

May

Sunday

FELT a lot better as the swifts have arrived, in full force, skimming a few inches above our heads. If it is warm enough for them then maybe the runner beans will feel quite comfortable.

★ ★ ★

I remember the swifts coming one particular summertime, returning once again to St. Barnabas church, to nest in the high, holy eaves. One got trapped inside during a morning service and seemed more bat than birdlike, swooping and blundering about, squeaking its distressed cry in the long shafts of summer sun. To us children it was a welcome if messy distraction! The church was just a short walk from our home, the cul-de-sac (sounds much nicer than "dead end"), with the great fir tree in the middle. The three-storey Edwardian homes with attics and cellars, had lovely long gardens joined on to other similar gardens, so that the view seemed to go on for ever. In fact our home's view went as far as Crystal Palace and I can remember being held up at the small attic window to see the glowing sky the night of the terrible fire. Maybe I do not really remember it first-hand but recall the telling, but I am nearly sure. I do recall quite clearly waiting for the twin towers to be demolished in the war. It had no particular meaning for one so young, just the mini drama of two grey shapes there, then not there. Now you see them, now you don't — the 'landmarks' gone for ever to be replaced by silver barrage balloons, our fat friends of the blitz. Sometimes one got away from its moorings and disappeared out of sight like a peacetime fete balloon, but without a name tag or prize for recovery.

★ ★ ★

I never went back to the house after the bomb fell down the road, destroying many buildings, badly damaging ours and the neighbours' in the cul-de-sac. I think I should have grieved less if I had gone with my parents and older sisters to help clear up the mess. I used to dream about it as it was, wander in and out of the rooms, slide down the banisters, (a fantasy never a fact), feeling a great sadness. The reality was the scarring of much of the familiar furniture in a strange house, (never "home" to me), great gashes caused by glass splinters patched up by our father as best he could. The beloved house was demolished quite recently alongside three others and blocks of flats have replaced them.

Our Number Six had been occupied by only two owners since ourselves and the last one was decidedly eccentric. I once had a chance to look down onto the garden that had been ours for so many happy years, from the house next door. We were walking home with Phil after going to one of the allotment annual shows. We decided to take a short cut through the churchyard. The round road where my home had been for fourteen years had another exit from its frying pan shape through St Barnabas' churchyard. This went past the flight of steps to the West door, (past the drooping crucified Christ-figure, life-size and realistic except for its creamy, deathly pallor, all a bit scary on the genuine wooden cross), out into another road. We were talking about the petition that was being prepared to prevent the demolition of these pleasant Edwardian houses with the inevitable replacement of blocks of flats. As we passed Number Four the woman in the garden looked up, probably overhearing us, and we got into conversation with her which led to an invitation inside.

It was a strange sensation, to be in the other half of our home, everything in reverse. In spite of this and the different contents I found it quite easy to imagine all those familiar pieces of furniture, pictures on the walls, the people who lived "next door" . . . us. As we went upstairs the memories became even clearer, "my nursery"; Daddy's dressing room; the attic where we used to play, the little window looking out over the suburban gardens over to SE 20. It was a shock to see the garden next door, once immaculate, cherished, now a wilderness, a great tangle of weeds, leggy shrubs, no order at all, only the walnut tree our father had planted remained. The neat herbaceous borders, striped lawn, the chestnut tree, all gone.

★ ★ ★

When I heard that the site had been cleared, the petition failing, I went up on my own to wander for a last time in what had been the loved garden and secure home. I remembered the garden shed which was part of the actual house structure, set under the scullery which had been our shelter during the war, sandbagged in, safe. That autumn my father worked away at filling the bags and I noticed great drops of sweat on his forehead as he ladled the heavy sand. It was something I had never seen before and it fascinated and worried me. He drank the cup of tea I had brought him, straightening himself, wiping away the sweat with his hankie. Up to then I had considered him God, now I was not so sure but maybe loved him even more.

On this last visit I found a piece of barley sugar edging from the vegetable plot area. These had framed all the cinder pathways containing the neat, well ordered rows of vegetables and fruits. Now this single piece is set into our top plot by the thornless blackberry, not doing anything really, is in fact, quite a nuisance when you mow the path. But it serves as a little reminder of a happy place where a love of growing things began, as I trailed behind dear Mr Watts, "helping", he ever patient with the little two-legged garden pest. I used to long for him to take off his hat as he had a perfect circle of snow-white hair around his pink pate . . . for me, bald was quite beautiful! In later years I was more useful and all the family did their share of "Digging for Victory".

Monday
Showers in the morning but it cleared up by the early afternoon so we had a chance to get all the bean sticks in and tied up, James thrusting them in, me, chopping off suitable lengths of string. The row higher up the plot supports the

climbing purple french beans, (harder to get), and this year James plans to have both purple and green climbers there. The low growing variety are so difficult to pick I find, getting terrible backache these days, ("Ageing is no picnic" agrees dear Lily) and the climbers seem to give a better yield per plant as well as being much easier to check and harvest.

One of the little apple trees is looking really sad, the Bramley, now four years old and should be doing better. Maybe it is because we allowed it to carry its splendid crop of huge green apples, all 14 of them! Perhaps it exhausted itself? We were too greedy and impatient we suspect. Anyway, if it goes on looking as sad as this we shall have to dig it up and replace it, but being us, we shall probably replant it, say a few kind words over it, and wait and see!

We are going to try and raise some mauve hellebore seedlings ourselves this year and have saved one of the flower-heads, letting it droop over a prepared flowerpot and securing it against strong winds or birds with a forked twig. Edith says that I ought to get lots of seedlings from all of our plants but then remembers that I am, according to her, "a Demon hoer . . . ".

Saturday
We enjoy the smell of bluebells in the park; and bruised mint and artemesia, as we clear around the top water tank. Tackled the thistley stuff which was given to us as an "artichoke", (globe-kind) but which has turned out otherwise. Beware of plotholders bearing unidentified "gifts"!

After so much rain the rhubarb is IMMENSE, huge stems, gorgeous pink ends.

The worms seem to be extra big and juicy too and the slugs, enormous but succumbing to the pellets, our last resort. All this wet, "should be growing rice" said Alf!

Much birdsong now. The courting trios of ducks fly low across the plots. Less song, more sounds from crows, magpies, jays, and our usual, smaller friendly ones, but no cuckoos at all so far. Another nice sound, the edging shears as they crunch through the grasses and buttercups, getting some order and line into our mini-meadows. Weeds, weeds, weeds!

★ ★ ★

Got quite hot working and my wellies felt all sweaty and horrid inside.

Mrs Somme has made her plot look positively neat and has put prickly holly twigs among her pea plants, says it props them up and keeps the mice away too.

The buttercups are really pretty but there really are too many. Sunny and Beattie were sitting up on their seat at the top, she looking rakish with his hankie knotted at the four corners protecting her head from the sunshine. They were enjoying the afternoon's warmth reflecting off the brick wall until a bee started buzzing too near Beattie's head. Thought she was waving to us at first so waved back cheerfully as she flapped away to rid herself of it!

Tuesday
Spinach due for the chop and the last leeks too. May leave some to flower for seed or "art".

The waterfall in the park must be big, could hear its roar above the usual plot and park sounds.

Mrs Somme is complaining of "something" eating her lettuce plants, not just pecking them but demolishing them completely it seems. Perhaps it is two-footed culprits as a pair of ducks have been enjoying their courtship on the plots and maybe fancy doing it in a ready-made "larder"?

Last year James disturbed two ducks in the avenue between the beansticks and the raspberry canes which flew away into the park. Two days later we found three duck eggs on top of our compost heap. We left them there but they were soon destroyed by a predator. Not too sad a happening as they were obviously abandoned by the parent birds.

Planted out the courgettes under cloches also gourds which we are training against a short wigwam of canes.

Tomato plants not at their best, not enough sunshine for them.

★ ★ ★

The new top plot gives us a very different perspective on things, sheltered as we are by the park fence and trees. We can look out towards the whole site right across to the houses and the two churches. The other afternoon we took up lemonade and biscuits and lay down on the car rug on the grass, (not quite "lawn" but improving with each cutting). We felt quite daring! It is perfectly private from the park as this section is totally filled with trees and blackberry bushes, so we can neither see in or be seen. It does smell a bit as the general compost heap is not far away but it is better than carbon monoxide and a good deal quieter than a suburban garden. No motor mowers, or transistors and the only time we see, (or hear), any of these is during a Test match or the last week of Wimbledon and then the owner seems a little sheepish and has it really low in volume. Some appreciate the second-hand contact however, with calls of "How many runs Fred?" . . . or "Light stopped play . . . ?" A headset is even less intrusive but when I tried mine it kept on falling off my belt and I gave up.

We do sometimes get the classics in the car park. The doctor (philosophical) has been known to leave his car door open, his tape of Vivaldi, Mozart and the like turned on to allow him to enjoy his weeding. As his plot is right beside the car park no one has cause for complaint, but his younger wife, German by birth, might prefer Wagner. In well fitting blue jeans she makes a colourful picture amongst the eschscholzia californica.

* * *

As we lie there, James says "This won't do" and falls asleep. I enjoy the rest too, remembering that only a year or two ago all this was a nettle patch, part covered with an old carpet, which in turn covered families of beetles and toads. Now it is our own precious retreat, and a refuge to overflow, shade-loving plants that need a home. Already we have a collection of all kinds of plants and shrubs cadged from, or offered to us, by like-minded gardeners. The two transplanted buddleias have survived their move and are in bud . . . the bees and butterflies will love them.

Wednesday
The onion seedlings have transplanted well and the corn looks good. Miriam was putting in actual runner bean plants today, that she had raised herself. James usually prefers to get them straight into the ground, planting some spares that he can remove later if all germinate. He assured her when she expressed doubts that hers would be fine. She complained that the snails had "gobbled up" several of the potted bean plants before she had spotted them. They do seem particularly energetic this year, achieving great heights, appearing at eye-level, disconcertingly, on the top raspberry canes!

Picked a nice big bunch of radishes from the row between the bean poles.

There seemed to be only us three up there this afternoon until we saw Winnie coming down the pathway with her wheelbarrow laden with vegetables and flowers.

"Been here since eleven!" she smiles,

pausing to greet us, rubbing the small of her obviously aching, broad back. I have lent her an old copy of a 1960's book published by the National Federation of Women's Institutes . . . "Wines, Syrups, & Cordials" and she says that she will pop in her version of the Elderflower Cordial when she returns it later. Evidently this recipe has proved very successful and we are promised a sample bottle.

Sunday
Edges . . . edges! Got them all done neatly taking it slowly. Now that James has chomped the sides down deeply with his sharp spade I can slide the shears along much more easily and do a far better job. It is still a little less than straight as you look down the length of the pathways, definitely serpentine, but if we lined these up, made them parallel I think we would end up with even stranger shaped plots!

Tuesday
There was quite a cold North East wind today but the sun shone and we gradually shed layers of clothing as we worked.

James once lost his favourite, (knitted by me) pullover this way, looping it over a beanpole and then forgetting it. He went up a few days later but it was gone.

As I weeded I noticed several selfsown nasturtium plants and made a mental note to take a couple home to plant in our Leeds chimney pot, the real thing rescued by our Yorkshire son-in-law! Last year I tried sowing some actual nasturtium seeds directly into the pot but they were pathetic and never flowered. Now James has put in a new liner and appropriate soil plus a new variegated ivy-plant. This must have got a headache though as during its first week there some four-footed creature hoicked it out leaving it halfwaydown the drive. James says it was the fox (as he got rid of its unwelcome calling cards also on the drive), but one wonders what it hoped to find for there was only a bit of homemade compost with the earth.

As I cleared weeds from around the rhubarb I noticed the ubiquitous jawbone!

It keeps reappearing, flat, grey-white, a row of efficient looking back teeth, just half of a whole. I flip it over with my hoe towards James who is weeding the onions, hoping he will bury it properly but pretty sure it will turn up again. Dog? . . . fox . . . ? we are not sure but it is a little gruesome, even though its colour proves its age.

As a child I had a terrible fear of skeletons, especially ones in impossible motion. The earliest conscious memory of the horrors of a skull is of a cartoon film seen during a seaside holiday visit to the cinema. I can remember the dark, the velvety seat, being small, everything big around me and the bright screen. Two naughty mice were playing around and at one point appeared each peeping out of the eye sockets of a skull on a shelf. For some reason I was terrified, which is strange because I must have been far too young to have realised the significance of bones and mortality.

I also remember a Sunday School session when a man addressed us children, telling us all about a valley "of bones". He described how the wind came and all these bones got up and joined together. To me this was quite a ghastly, nightmareish image and far from inspiring anything but terror!

However, I think I must have contained my reaction as there is no family story of Nell disgracing herself yet again!

Then there was this book, a great heavy encyclopedia with a blue cover. In it was a section which described the actions of the spine and it was illustrated with two pictures of skeletons, one carrying a pile of boxes, the other seated at a piano. I would sit on the floor with the book, turning the pages slowly, dreading the point when I would reach this page but drawn to do it . . . early signs of masochism?

My older sisters would scoff at "the baby" even teasing me with a particular gramophone record of Gracie Fields singing, "Ain't it grand to be blooming well dead!" Halfway through this side the music stopped and bony xylophone noises were made and clickings which were supposed to be our Gracie taking out her teeth and cracking her bones, noises I couldn't bear!

"You are not playing THAT record" I would plead suspicious of their reassurances and concealment of the label. The wound-up nursery gramophone played on while I tried to retreat, only to find a sisterly hand firmly holding the ribbed brass door handle, preventing my escape!

My ally at that tender time was my father who seemed to understand my distress at the illustration of Pilgrim and the lions barring his way. Later, my need to cover over a reproduction of a Grunewald crucifixion with its grey flesh and terrible thorns was accepted so I was able in time to uncover the image and cope with the sadness without losing any sensitivity.

I cannot understand how, people actually choose to look at horror films, find them entertaining! But I am delighted that there is now a charming and quite unterrifying children's cartoon with its main characters . . . skeletons! Maybe I shall watch these with the grandchildren and lay my own ghosts.

Thursday
There is a patch of ground elder by the lower water tank, I must get it all out

before I plant my clump of selfsown Welsh poppies there. The leaves are very similar so I must warn James so that he doesn't hoick out the seedlings thinking them weeds. Hitched the strings around the delphiniums higher, one spike is already in full bloom. This is only their second year and they are growing really well. The piece of the plot that James has let me have for flowers is developing as I planned, into a typical English herbaceous border. There isn't enough room at home but here, in my own patch I can fulfil a dream!

I was saddened to see the mutilation of the lupins by greenfly. The buds are completely covered, all the flowerheads crawling. The spraying we had to do obviously came too late and I shall have to cut all three plants right down, they look such a mess. It is a pity as the flowers would have been pink and cream and two kinds of purple. Maybe there is just a chance they will recover, possibly have late summer flowers but I rather doubt it.

Planted out the sweet pea seedlings in the gap by the loganberry and used the wires for supports with a few extra strings. We ended up with only a few plants as some were lost when we were away for a few days, coming up more quickly than anticipated and getting thwarted by the covering glass. Some did a U-turn and disappeared but we saved the less ambitious ones, gently mounding the fine soil around them until they grew stronger and straighter. I hope that they will reward our loving care with some nice, sweet-scented blooms.

I am not likely to compete with Percy's usual splendid show but I shall enjoy the scent of our modest row as I pick the summer fruits.

A rogue hollyhock has appeared by the runner bean-poles, "Shall I leave it?" asks James. I say "Yes" as although I have quite a nice collection in my patch I have yet to own a white or lemon one. There are beautiful pinks of all kinds, plum, burgundy and magenta, even a pale caramel one, but no whites. Maybe this odd one will be just that although I do hear that seedlings are rarely true to parents. I believe this, for friends, knowing my wish for lemon or white, give me seeds from their flowers, convinced I shall be as lucky as they are. If all fails this year, I shall take up kind Lily's offer of an actual piece of parent plant and see if it will stand the move from one end of the site to the other.

Saturday
Meg was just leaving the site as we arrived mid-morning.

"Just off for a quick hair-do" she told us, "Makes me sing better".

It appeared that her church choir was giving a concert that evening and that a wedding preceded it. Nevertheless she thought that she might find the time to return to her plot between events. What dedication!

She said that her sister, a hair expert, groaned at Meg's lack of proper "style" and we discussed the value of a good cutter discovering that we shared the same hairdresser.

"Knows what to do with short hair" we agreed.

The sky began to blacken in the afternoon but the rain held off until teatime so maybe Meg achieved her extra work without getting her hair-do spoiled.

James spotted a stranger helping himself to mint and parsley from Percy's plot.

"Percy all right?" he asked him, a tactful way of saying who are you and what are you doing!

The reply was that Percy was away on holiday in Germany and we told him that we were off there ourselves soon, to visit our son and family.

Saw a male chaffinch on the lower plot. There seem to be far fewer of these nowadays. I can remember them being quite common once, now it is quite an event to spot one.

Picked rhubarb, parsley and a fistful of radishes.

Monday
Mostly hoeing today and a bit of edgeing. The grass is growing fast now and James plans to borrow the motor mower next weekend. Now he uses our hand one which used to keep some bowling green immaculate. Its present job must give it a culture shock, as James struggles up and down the bumpy narrow pathways,

the broader flatter sweeps are few and far between. This poor, refined mower now has to cope with something more akin to an irregular rock-hard switchback than a velvet, banded "green".

Returned for a bite to eat and James had a well-earned snooze in front of the cricket on TV. A flower pressing session for me, my therapy! This time I had not forgotten my picked flowerheads . . . poached egg flowers, (excellent for pressing), some of the next door plot's pansies; some early marigolds, the common sort. These yellows and oranges are the best colours, never disappointing you but I have low expectations of any blues or mauves; and the scarlets, like poppies, become a faded maroon. Most leaves if not too fleshy press well, keeping their colour and even the disgusting, bloated-rooted weed that invades both our garden and plot, supplies a pleasing trefoil leaf. One piece of the leaf is a perfect heart-shape so comes in useful for February 14th or special greetings!

The feverfew leaves are a brilliant yellow-green so were included in today's pressing but I fear I squashed a few blackfly at the same time. The pressing made the leaves smell very rank but I expect this will pass and not spoil the delights of uncovering my work in weeks to come. I love the moment of lifting up the blotting paper to reveal the fine papery shapes, the delicate colours and patterns, the unreduced brilliance of some of the petals . . . more nice surprises than dismay usually.

* * *

Later drove over to Wychvale Garden Centre to look at fruit trees but while we were there got caught in a terrible rainstorm. It did not last long but was fierce and we had to take shelter in the covered, pelargonium area. The air was so damp and heavy inside that James said he felt like someone in an H E Bates' novel! The scent of the flowers, the smell of warm earth was cloying, sickly. We missed our cup of tea as by the time the shower had left off, the cafe had put up the "Closed" sign, even though there were luckier people than us inside still.

We felt headachey and peeved and

dumped our empty trolley where it was, leaving treeless as we had not found anything suitable before the rains came.

We would pass another garden centre on our route home but we watched the sky warily as we drove, were those heavy slatey clouds following us? But we were luckier this time, both in weather and trees, finding at the second place a half standard Bramley, a nice shape, reasonably priced and just what we wanted. I stocked up with crystallized ginger while James queued up at the check-out . . . (funny place for ginger but it is better there and much cheaper than the Health Food Shop's kind). With a little gentle bending here and there we managed to tuck our new tree into the car and drove directly to the allotments beating the following rain. The site was locked up so it meant the usual performance with the stiff padlock. There must have been rain there earlier, maybe part of our deluge, as the leaves of the alchemilla mollis were beautiful with their crystal droplet beads. I always wonder why these particular leaves have this charming character . . . they do not seem at all oily, quite the contrary, their green surface seems soft to the touch, but the water gathers and collects in this particular way, very pleasing.

Dug a hole and dropped in our new tree in its container to await proper planting later.

One good thing had come out of our first abortive visit and that was to identify a plant someone had given to James. He had put it in "my" patch and I had grudgingly allowed it to stay but would prefer to have been asked! He did not know what it was so I could not position it properly re colour or height. It seems that it is a Tillima so now I can look it up in our Readers Digest gardening bible and decide on its fate.

Tuesday
Brought an angelica leaf home last night to gentle the stewed rhubarb but it must have fallen off the basket as we decanted the car, as I found it limp and sad in the driveway this morning. I still have not tried crystallizing the stems. The recipes I read are so long drawn out that I don't think I have the patience to try them out,

and anyway, when do I really need it!

The best method was the one I found in my battered Good Housekeeping manual, as old as our marriage having been given to us as a gift by a school friend. One half is "Household" the other "Cooking". The first has hints on regular Spring cleaning regimes; how to clean your boiler; tarnished silver problems; silver fish and so on, but it is not quite as irrelevant as James' lovely old copy of Mrs Beeton. Another battered volume in need of repair too but full of delights. I just enjoy looking at the line engravings; the hectic, tinted formal table-layings; the sumptuous dishes; reading the recipes which must have given their consumers much indigestion surely . . . ("For indigestion remedies turn to page 128")!

Betty's more realistic book has proved more practical though, especially in our early married days as I had only cooked breakfasts in my single state, or student snacks. Wartime frugality did not encourage childish experiments in the kitchen and the days of dried egg and ration books were not so very far away. Added to this, an education completely lacking in any form of "Domestic Science" you have one very unskilled newlywed!

James remembers all too vividly those first meals shared after a day's work in London. Now you would have popped into M & S on the way home, picking up, (if you could afford it) some aptly named "convenience" foods. Then, I had to learn my culinary skills by trial and error and trust that if the way to a man's heart really was his stomach, that my marriage would survive James' indigestion and fond memories of my mother-in-laws excellent cooking! (So much for the "New Man" in the nineteen fifties!)

Friday
Back from a family visit to Broadstairs. Sunny day and a fresh almost cold breeze, but we sat in the garden and enjoyed a splendid lunch with Alec and Peg. They have a gorgeous white rhododendron shrub which we admired, pink budded but the purest of whites when out fully. They originally grew it at their previous home in Cornwall but had brought it with them to Kent a few years ago.

The soil is not suitable so they have made a sturdy square raised bed and filled it with appropriate soil. Now the shrub, with accompanying azaleas, flourish in their seaside home. We have asked them to try and layer us a piece but of course this will take some time and goodness knows where we will put it if successful! There was a lovely montana clematis too, romping all over a nearly-dead plum tree, with a wonderful show of blossom. After lunch Leo (dog) dropped a lot of noisy hints that it was much more fun to have his ball thrown on the beach rather than in the more restricting space of the garden, so we gave in and went for a bracing walk on the sands.

Saturday
Planted the new Bramley properly moving the sad older one to the back of the plot for a second chance maybe. James gave the new one a good dollop of well rotted compost to get its roots into and with some watering and praying for better luck this time left it to settle in.

Had a row over the new asparagus bed! I had taken four (asking to be eaten) spears from the bed at different points and had got ticked off by an irate James who said that I "had ruined them!". However, when we got home I checked in two gardening books and each said that it was quite permissable to take a shoot or two from single clumps during the first year. He would not apologise and I ate them!

Last evening there was a great thunderstorm with a sudden great rush of wind so fierce that it knocked some of James' precious Bonsais off their staging, no breakages or real damage luckily. The trees and shrubs in the garden were whipped and flattened but although the raindrops were huge they were not actual hailstones thank goodness.

I had noticed from the kitchen window before the storm, the two young brown blackbirds importuning their weary parents for more food. Then one came to sip water from the dish, deciding then to take a bath, (better in that order I suppose). There was hardly any water in the dish so I went out with a saucepanful and topped it up for him. From the window watched him return to have a marvellous time, splashing and fluttering, his head thrown back in apparent ecstasy, his yellow bill still young and gapey.

Another observation from my window recently, was of a starling. He had found a piece of dry toast, a tasty breakfast relic indeed, but a day's exposure had hardened it, so he brought it across to the water dish, and dunked it!

The rainstorm did no damage up the plot luckily but we were glad that we had staked and tied our new tree well. My flowerpatch looked a bit forlorn but better than I had expected perhaps partly due to the new plastic ringed supports I had for my birthday. These allow the bushier plants to grow up through the holes but are unobtrusively green and soon hidden by the foliage.

The garden looks its best in the Spring but I have lots of tubs and pots of geraniums for summer colour and the lavender is always a joy. But we enjoy the white hydrangeas; creamy sorbaria; spikes of acanthus and yet more hollyhocks! We once had a neighbour in the Close who declared that "Hollyhocks didn't seem quite right here . . . " Funny man . . . what ever is "right"?

He did not seem to object to our irises though and the bed is even bigger now. We asked Winnie why we had so few flowers last year and she told us that they must be overcrowded and that you had periodically to dig them up and divide them. We did this last year and she gave us some tubers from her own collection on the plot. Lovely names . . . Sable Night; Cleo; Chartreuse. It turns out though that she had been too generous and had given all of one variety to various friends. I suspect it was one that bloomed singly this year, a gorgeously scented one, almost white. Of course I have offered to return it to her but she says, not to worry, Meg had an even bigger root she thinks, and can spare a piece more easily.

Tuesday

Oh the agonies of leaving home and plot for a holiday!

So much to do, so much to organise.

"Is it worth it?" grumbles James trying to sort out watering schedules. The end of May is not too bad a time though but no time is entirely trouble free allotment-wise and this year the worry is the care of the newly planted tomatoes. However, Phil, bless her heart, has promised to keep a weather eye on them and water if necessary, at least they are near the top tank.

I am more concerned with things domestic and leave the allotment worries to James. At the worst it will be a little weedy on our return and anyway, we are only away for six days!

June

Wednesday

HOME again and all is well. Evidently it was pretty dry the early part of the week but much rain fell towards the end, really heavy, so we returned to a garden and allotment looking quite green and happy in spite of our absence.

When we were children, our home-coming was not complete until my father had fetched back Tiddles, our marmalade cat from his cattery holiday home. Released from his travelling basket he would prowl around the whole house from floor to floor, room to room until his inspection was completed, and all the time yowling! Only then would he settle down and allow us to pet him, let us children make a fuss of him while he head-butted us, purring now. We would make him an excuse to postpone the unpacking all too willingly!

Sunday

Beattie had found a ripe red strawberry today and announced the fact as she passed us by the rhubarb patch. Promised to give her my recipe for a nice rhubarb pudding as she said that she only pickled it as the family didn't like it as a sweet usually. Maybe they will like this battery, orangey one.

Saw a female duck land heavily in Mrs Somme's plot. It waddled about and had a good drink from the lid of a cold frame. Considering that it lives on the fresh water of the lake in the park and nearby stream, it seemed a little odd, but then we thought that it might contain some special quality, or taste better when taken from a pane of glass?

Very sunny but a lovely breeze. A full to capacity car park and everyone busy. The weeds are really stuck in and hoeing is hard work. Did the edges but was sad to cut down the buttercups, they are so bright. All looks well at the moment but weedy after our spell away.

It rained later, lightning and thunder crashes and then really heavy rain, just right for the things put in today.

Put in the cane supports for the tomatoes. Picked about 10 pounds of gooseberries I should think and got the usual scratched arms above the rubber gloves.

The runner beans are only a few inches high but have scarlet flowers already.

James has built his own patent wind-break round the tomato patch, sheets of old ridged plastic secured with canes pushed down well either side. He can then slide the sheets out when he wants to get inside to pick off shoots or water.

The birds are having a go at the compost mulch scattering it all over the place. The manure is full of fat pink worms and a great larder for them. Our robin came so close today, perching on the wheelbarrow's handle waiting for the tasty bits to appear as we shifted the muck. Probably has young to feed.

The paths are untidy again and need a concerted effort of spade, edging tool and shears.

Planted out cabbage and Brussel sprouts and netted them well against pigeons and their like.

Monday am
Went up in the week in the daytime by myself as James away in Wales. Different people there then. Eddie working hard with a bit of leave, "trying to catch up". He is so pleased with his raspberries, a mass of flowers and looking really healthy but is concerned that his whole plot is not dug over and planted out. Says when he is retired like many of the plotholders are, we will see great things from him!

Two of the allotment committee members were there too getting trestle tables out of the shed with a lot of noise and heavy sighing. They seemed to be checking and repairing them. Surely we are not nearing "showtime" already?

Tuesday
Watered. The gourds look a bit sad and floppy but the tomatoes are enjoying their mulch and seem a lot perkier now. They are greener too whereas the surplus plants in the garden are positively anaemic in comparison.

Lily offered me some lettuces and a cup of coffee, and as ours are up but not yet big enough to pick, and a break welcome, was glad to accept both. She has a garden that backs onto the plot that she runs so well. Her garden is as delightful as its owner with apple and pear trees, perennials, annuals, smooth grassy bits and interesting angles and corners, all beautifully kept. Everything looks so cherished but not 'cultivated' overly, my own idea of a perfect garden. Told me that our grey shrub is a santolina and that we must cut it right down, really fiercely each spring or it will get woody.

★ ★ ★

Made a batch of Aunt Alice's rhubarb chutney and sampled some although you are supposed to leave it to mature. The ginger makes it quite hot but James (who says that he can't stand ginger!) has had two great dollops so obviously did not notice it.

Used some of the gooseberries for jam and gave Phil some for her mint jelly. She always apologises for using it for the jelly but what does it matter? See that they are 66 pence in the shops.

Thursday

Evening visit to the plot. The delphiniums grace the car park end and the bright orange of the marigolds were catching the late sun. The blues of the delphiniums have been really varied and I am cutting off the dead flowerheads in the hope that we shall have a second flush of spikes later in the summer. One of the plants, the last to flower, is the tallest of the group and still has quite a good collection of blooms at the top. I shall leave these as long as I can but have taken home some of the seed heads to dry. I think that they might be interesting for a winter mixture. I suspended them over the bath on the line and the next day found a natural catchment area for masses of tiny black seeds! I swept them up carefully and put them in a clear marked envelope and popped them in the fridge with the packet of Pansy seeds to "stratisfy". (I think that is the description James gives to the conditioning of his Bonsai seeds when he gives them an artificial, out-of-season wintering in the fridge).

* * *

The scattering of all these blue petals in my flower patch has deceived me several times with thinking that I have discovered a piece of broken china, only to find that I am picking up a soft fallen petal! Many years ago we encouraged the children to help us collect any piece of coloured china found in gardens, our own or other peoples, sometimes fields, cherishing the hope that one fine day we would have enough material to make a unique paving stone, or a tile-topped garden table. The collection exists, somewhere up in the loft and I still collect pieces wondering always why they are, predominately, blue?

★ ★ ★

Stole some of Ruth's Love-in-the-Mist seedpods for drying and ate two of her ripe Mange Tout peas, very sweet and scrunchy. Have been buying ours from the supermarket, the produce of Zimbabwe!

Monday
Only the odd really hot days. Things seem dry and it has been quite cold but

not wet for a while now. Pleased with the broad bean crop and the gooseberries but it is a funny kind of summer — still to come though the days will inevitably shorten from now on . . . so much for "midsummer"!

Lily showed us the chicken-wire compost heap on her neighbour's plot, full of dried grasses and bits, and the robin's nest in it about halfway up. The bird used to fly in through the hexagonal spaces and feed the just visible chicks. Lily was keeping watch on the family as when the owner returned from holiday she might unknowingly wreck the home. She usually leans her bike against the support too, just by the nest area, but with a neighbourhood watch, all will probably be well and the rubbish will go elsewhere until the family has flown.

Tuesday
Someone has asked us if we know an elderflower champagne recipe. We did, but had forgotten it, probably because we had tried it ourselves the year before and had produced some undrinkable muck! Maybe we had not sterilised the

111

bottles enough. James had tasted some brewed up by others more expert than us obviously, and found it really good. There is a splendid flower crop up by the car park gate, plenty for all but not for us thank you!

★ ★ ★

Have found my Wine & Cordials book safely slung in a Safeways bag on the raspberry stake, plus a thank you note from Winnie also inside, and a big bottle of her Elderflower Cordial with recipe. It uses 25 flowerheads and oranges and lemons with quite a bit of sugar. "Dilute with water and ice as soon as you like" the note says . . . "and for the rest of the summer . . . if it lasts that long". It smells nice anyway. Mrs Somme says you can scatter the little flowerlets on stewed or fresh fruit and it adds a nice flavour, should have no failure with that surely.

Friday
A scorcher for about ten days in a row — always extremes. Plants wilt, the watering can has broken after long

service so we have bought a lighter plastic replacement. Now with one each we can cope better. Plot productive but weedy and shaggy. "Judgement Day" looms again but we are not urged as in past years under the watchful eye of the previous Hon. Sec., with many little notices, to "pay attention to paths and verges please".

A whole day's work done including the final patch to be dug over. Surely a record for lateness? The runner beans got a spray of soapy water to discourage the black fly. James dug up the 'extra' plants from the middle of the rows and is putting them around a wigwam of canes for it seems a pity to waste them and there is plenty of space.

Saturday
Mrs Somme was dressing her redcurrants with London Tan tights, bemoaning the necessity, and the greedy damage done by the birds. The earth under the bushes was freckled with green unripe berries. We talked about the Tradescant Trust in Lambeth, the Museum of Garden History. I wonder if there is a history

of allotmenteering?

The magpies were making a terrible noise all afternoon. Maybe there was an owl in the trees and they were barracking it?

Picked several more pounds of gooseberries although I had thought to have cleared the bushes the other evening. I have discovered a pot of gooseberry and apple jam which I love almost as much as marmalade, and it was dated three years ago! Not a speck of mould though and quite delicious.

Giving the rhubarb a rest from picking now but got some nice hearty lettuces. The paths look better as James has been working really hard at them because of the dreaded imminent Borough 'inspection' week. Heard the tale of the plotholder who regularly wins prizes with his flower beds. He evidently pops out the morning of the judging and BUYS his geraniums if his own reared ones don't look up to scratch!

Not interested in awards at all, just grow to eat and enjoy being plotholders, but James did once get a novice prize way back, think it was for onions. Certainly this year they are splendid, particularly the ones he has grown from seed. So proud he even photographed them for the album!

Sunday
Still very warm and humid. Alf's old dog is feeling the heat too as he urges it up the path on the end of a long piece of knotted rope. If he stops to talk, the dog ambles on until out of line and then flops down wherever he is regardless of place. He has been known to relieve himself after much preliminary sniffing and selecting, on a clump of chives, or seedlings so a plastic bag is sometimes brought along later to remove the offending pile and we all wash well our salad stuff and herbs! The foxes probably spray too so such hygienic actions are necessary. The dog lumbers up the pathway followed by a kindly cursing Alf with, "get on you silly bugger", and apologies for his straying, "can't see, got cataract, silly idiot . . . " but all this with much affection. Some days he is left in Alf's van, sitting in the passenger seat, bolt upright like one of the stone Chinese lions at Kew, watchful with

his near blind eyes, patient, dreaming doggy dreams, very smelly but obviously well loved.

* * *

The bouncy black and white dog, a mere juvenile compared with Alf's, lives over at the town houses and today accompanied the young owner, dragging him along impatiently on his lead. The man had a great pile of tools and boxes and all these came near to toppling as they made their way up the path to their plot. He has taken over from the couple both plot and house together it seems.

The previous couple had worked together on their plot rather spasmodically, providing a great sight in the high summer, sporting yachting cap, short shorts, bare pectorals (he); she, when the weather suited, wore the tiniest of bikinis, the briefest of shorts, but they were very fair-weather gardeners and only graced the site when the sun shone. They also had a dog a small white poodle, somehow right for them. It never came over to the site but sat on their first floor balcony observing them from across the road. One summer's day we were treated to a fine sight. The woman evidently wanted a pre-holiday full tan so stood naked by the balcony window, her back turned to the morning sun. I don't know how many people in the car park noticed her that day, but I think quite a few plotholders worked facing that direction, perhaps hoping that she would revolve as the day wore on. It is possible that she was modelling for an artist, "Nude against the light" but I think unlikely. The disabled lady in the car park was treated to this display facing, as she was, the window in question, but she preferred to read her newspaper. I doubt that she told her husband when he returned from his labours in case he got over excited.

Tuesday
Got all excited ourselves watching a TV gardening programme about water gardens, in particular how to convert a large ceramic, (holed) pot into a watertight container. But in the end we both decided that it was a bit of an apology for a "pond" proper

and that if we couldn't have the real thing, the tinkle of running water, the lily pads, perhaps it was better not to get involved with half measures. Anyway James quite rightly said that we have enough general paraphanalia filling our small garden already . . . tubs galore, seedlings, Bonsais, garden seats (two), not forgetting the essential potting shed, lean-to greenhouse and compost maker!

James dreams of a "real" walled garden but I suppose we should have to have the house with it and that's a bit beyond our means. I say we ought to hunt around for a derelict mansion and buy just the relic of the garden and restore it, wouldn't that be wonderful? But not too far away for how could we part with our plots!

Winnie told me that she was evacuated to a manor house down in Devon which had a lovely walled garden, as "big as this . . . ", (an expansive wave embracing most of the site described its vastness).

It had little low box hedges, espalier fruit trees, all a bit gone to seed but nice, and there were stables and a pony. Obviously this part of Winnie's war was not over traumatic and maybe it was this pleasant childhood experience that set her young feet onto the path of the true gardener.

Tonight, it must be a record for Winnie had been up there working since eleven! She is rosy with exertion and tired understandably. She said that she helped herself as instructed, to some of our ripe gooseberries while we were away, about an ice cream box-ful, could she pay me? Of course I said "No" but added that I had a charity collection box and was immediately given a generous £4!

The vixen trotted close by James and he called out "where's your bag?" as she had something in her mouth, but I had left it in the car. Brief panic when we got home as James thought that he had lost his special (ancient) gardening gloves but we found them safe under a huge lettuce in my basket. The lettuces need to be picked every day now or they'll bolt so I am able to be very choosy only using the best hearty bits. The rest becomes compost so nothing is wasted.

Must take the shears up next visit as the top area by the park fence is a bit shaggy. The kerria (nicely named

"Batchelor's Buttons") has taken and looks established now which is good, but I ought to be clearing away the long grass and weedy bits around it. There is a new obnoxious weed up there which sticks to your clothes and skin, not like individual burrs but the actual leaves and stems drag at you with their great long swathes.

Friday pm
Tonight the swifts were flying really low, almost head-height. They skim and swoop silently and we are reminded that it will not be too long before they depart again, all too soon. The plot is almost all dug over now and looks pretty trim. The newly deep-chopped edges make it much tidier.

Planted the gourds and the last of the sprouts. The angelica is in full flower and over five feet tall already. Did a vigorous hoe but hard on the shoulder as the ground is very sticky. Saw a motionless golden toad near the raspberries, a good size and really beautiful.

The slim mauve (Siberian?) irises are in bloom down at the bottom of the plot, they like it there, very damp usually but not much sunlight there, except in the early part of the day. The beans, runner and french look healthy, in fact the whole plot is pretty fair now. We picked some broad beans catching them just right as they are not too strongly-flavoured at this stage. Found another use for them in salad. You steam them first and then strip off the grey coats and toss them with the dressing and other salad bits. I wish I liked their taste as well as their look, sadly I do not.

The spinach is really over. Last week I picked the still-tender top leaves and some small side ones and cooked them very slightly, tasted good but the rest has gone to seed now. Uncovered all the clochéd lettuces which are large, beautiful and green, but a bit limp and leathery I thought. Not popular when I said that I preferred the supermarket's crisper Dutch ones!

Saturday
Very hot. Sat and drank lots of diet lemonade in the shady patch by the hellebores. James takes off his wellies to air his soggy feet and for the umpteenth

time I tell him that he ought to get himself a pair of lighter shoes for summer work, or, relegate an old pair of walking shoes. He agrees as usual and does nothing, typically husband-like.

Christopher Robin calls across to us asking if we like the weather.

"Yes" answers James, "but I wish I was watching myself working!"

I thought this rather clever and tried to imagine it!

I didn't hurry back to continue picking the raspberries hoping that a patch of shade from the park trees would make its way over the area soon. A lovely day for school fetes, garden parties and weddings too. There had already been two lots of bell-ringing so some couples were lucky. "Happy the bride on whom the sun shines" the saying goes . . . which seems sad for all those others!

The angelica is all tattered majesty now, the great seedheads dark against the sky from where we sit in our resting place. Seen from the car park end they appear pale brown and grey-green against the dark sycamores and holly.

Sunday
Bill and Cissie were going home having
had enough of the heat. The grandchildren were with them, flushed and
getting tetchy. They had come up to
"help Grandpa" ostensibly, but it was
nearing midday so all were packing up.
Their mother, fourth on the way, looked
as if she would give birth on the spot.
The littlest girl would soon have to give
up her status but she seems a baby still
herself.

Cissie told us a nice story, how last
summertime the youngest grandchild had
become really fretful, then a babe in arms
still, and Cissie had carried her up to the
wild top part of the site. She sat down
in the cool on a fallen tree trunk and
began to sing to the child a soothing
song, cuddling her. A slight noise made
her look up to see sitting quite close by,
one of the foxcubs, its head cocked on
one side, apparently enjoying the human
music and peace!

Wednesday
Went up early evening although the sky
looked very black in parts. Had terrific

123

hail storm yesterday so was a little wary. The soil was really sticky, black and really hard work. Went up and down the rows of beetroot seedlings, hoeing carefully, also the leeks and two rows of french beans. Took a photograph before the light went of the angelica flowers towering above everything.

Only a couple of people there. Had to smile at Mrs Somme's plot. Not only are there two derisive gloves upended on sticks (to deter what — whom?) but the latest additions are pairs of tights, still with their gussets but footless, making improper flesh-coloured 'V'-signs on the current bushes. The fruiting stems are rammed into each 'leg' and the whole scene has a decidedly rakish air!

A threatening black sky remained only a threat and I was able to get home dry before the clouds opened.

Friday
Robby was cutting the long grass in the car park when we arrived. For once the sky was fairly bright and the dark clouds pushed eastwards by a much kinder wind. He had a little noisy petrol-driven

affair. We could make good use of it on our paths. James has cut the edges yet again but it is always a bit like painting the Forth Bridge, never ending.

★ ★ ★

There are gaps in the beetroots rows, not sure why. Picked two really hearty lettuces and made some lettuce soup with the outer leaves. This time I just dropped shredded leaves into the blender with some basic stock and added a little milk. It turned out a beautiful speckled green.

Lovely clouds this evening, soot and cream and a good dramatic sunset for a change.

Saturday
Almost a total allotment day, and a day marked by flowers. It was only broken by a sandwich lunch and a quick visit to the primary school's annual fair. No smell of overcooked beefburgers this year, but once again the usual sounds and sights; loud Tannoyed music and blurry announcements; children with painted

faces, streaked hair, strange cat creatures and elfin make-up. Balloons escaped and got caught up in the wind disappearing over the allotments across the way, (not our site).

The school had been built where the wartime plots used to be. Uncle Bill played his part in "digging for victory" and he offered the young James a piece of his own allotment to cultivate. It turned out to be a bomb crater thirty feet across! Now it grows crops of bright-eyed infants and leggy juniors. Today at the fair some of these had already become too dignified to be seen hurtling about on the inflatable bouncing castle, showing their knickers.

★ ★ ★

James tried a lucky dip at Mary's stall and found his plastic egg contained a pair of false red lips! We then spent some considerable time picking up pieces of blue and white polystyrene which filled the dip basket as the wind had been blowing it all over the playing field. The Punch and Judy man came out front at the end of his performance and after a lot of question and answer, and a bit of a conjure, produced a real live white rabbit. A gentle conclusion to a tale of violence. Alison, still just an "infant", neat in navy and white, sucked on a bendy straw, looking away from the cruel pantomime, frowning a little under the well cut fringe. Last year she had happily shouted with the rest at Mr Punch's antics, now she was less sure of the joke, preferring to keep her distance, observing other things from her seat on the wooden rhino in the infant's playground.

A little boy had lost his mother and wept soggily, refusing our comfort, but a teacher came to his rescue and soon the message calling for the parent, blared out competing with the Cadet band. Earlier, the school orchestra had given a performance in the hall. Children making music are always a lovesome thing and this day, no less. There were recorders and flutes, some very small violinists, and more unusually, a couple of cellists. A girl percussionist kept up the beat with a smile that never left her face the whole time and the adult pianist and conductor guided their flock to a triumphant encore of "Land of Hope and Glory" written for three parts. We applauded loudly, the children gave short, jerky bows to us and we joined the long queue for tea and a biscuit for twenty pence.

★ ★ ★

Before the fair we had gone to the plot intent on tackling the edges. We took an old but sharp spade worn rounded with much use. I followed on picking up the clods of grass and finishing off the job with the edging shears. These had been unusable for a while as a spring had gone and the two parts separated. We asked around and eventually found that you could write to somewhere in Wales for a replacement. We posted off the bits and in a short time received the parts and a bill for less than two pounds! Now they worked as well as ever and we did most of the main paths before retreating home in the rain. It was lunchtime or thereabouts anyway. Neither of us were wearing watches but the Parish called the hours also our stomachs.

Percy was there too having his alternate well-paced periods of labour and rests.

He retires for a smoke sitting in his alcove of elm and sycamore almost hidden. His mate seems to have disappeared and the second chair is empty. It is in an even poorer state than Peter's which is saying much as there is little remaining of the fabric, just frayed strips of plastic over the rusting frame. However, he seems comfortable enough, relaxed, legs wide apart, his smoking hand elegantly raised in a Noel Coward gesture. I had admired his sweet peas soon after we arrived and he asked Colin if he might give "his good lady" a bunch to take home. Permission given, I was grateful to accept the neat posy and all I had to do when I got home was to place them in a small pottery jug just as they were. He had commented that the stems were short, "Still" I said, "you are not competing for a silver trophy are you" . . . "Heaven forbid" he laughed, being one of us, a non-competitive spirit. In their pot they scented the whole kitchen all day smelling of honey and almonds. In the evening it seemed such a pity to drown this scent with our first cooking of Spring cabbage so I moved them into the sitting room.

Our second visit after the fair got the edges finished and then we divided our labours, James to weed the cabbage patch and I to pick more gooseberries. Winnie came past us on her way to the car park, her day's work done, and greeted us. We asked her if she had any more shade-loving plants for our 'extension' by the park fence and she said that she would like to walk up to see it. It is all very new still, just a beginning but she appreciated this, inviting us to come up and see her own special patch. Even after all these years there are parts of the allotment site that we rarely visit so we laid down tools gladly and went up to the top with her. She has two plots, one a neat vegetable and flower garden, the other a patch under some trees right up in the corner. There had been a big house and shrubbery alongside the wall previously, but last year the house came down and the flats went up and light was let in. The "prestigious" block was not too close and preferable to the dark trees and shrubs. The plants seemed to respond to Winnie's loving care and she has shaped the area into a place which positively glows with health. Broom, iris, herbs, small shrubs thrive with her attention and obvious skills. At the edge, the sunnier part, were some self-sown cornflowers in every shade of blues and pinks, even a lovely dusky mauve one. She responded to my admiration by picking me a huge bunch which ended up in another vase beside Percy's sweet peas. She too had received a bunch from him and was reminded of days long ago when she worked in a florists'. The delivery of the seasonal blooms was a scented memory as the black tissue paper was removed layer by layer and the flowers taken out of their box.

Her vegetables were short thick rows, peas, broad beans, healthy seedlings of turnip and carrot and the strawberry patch bright with fruits. One part was well netted, the other, "left for the blackbirds" she said.

We walked back together, she commenting on our busier area, preferring the quiet of the more secluded plots she had. "You don't have to talk" she said but she always talks to us and seems cheerful, rosy cheeked, freckled, not at all a recluse. She trundled the wheelbarrow down the path to the car saying she felt hungry. "Don't ask me what we are having" I said, "for I don't know!" She said she fancied fish and chips but was too scruffy to go into the shop. She called back to us had we heard about the bees? Evidently there had been a swarm in the afternoon, a great black living mass clinging to Mrs Ackroyd's fruit-cage pole. She didn't know if they had been collected or if either of the bee-keeper's had been told but they had gone somewhere anyway.

★ ★ ★

I rather fancy one of the beemen, not the younger family-man but the more mature one! Yesterday we returned from a few days away and on the way home called in on the plot to review the weeds and crops situation. There were a lot of loganberries ready to pick and several bolting lettuces.

The beeman was completing some chores going to and fro with the wheelbarrow and I was by our car hunting for something to put the loganberries in, unsuccessfully. James was watering the tomatoes as it had not rained enough whilst we were away. I enquired about his bees. While he answered me I observed what nice hands he had as he stripped off his gloves. Maybe it is all those zips on his white overalls that attract me! I suspect though I am probably old enough to be his mother!

I am listening though, and learn about the act of swarming. It all seems highly complicated but understood that the old queen bee excretes a substance that supresses the gene that might allow too many rival queens to be bred, how clever. He said that a swarm can be the result of overcrowding not necessarily "rival" queens. He expects swarm activity roundabout now and had got his first emergency call last week about the swarm on the fruitcage pole. He had been unable to get to the site so it was the younger man who came, arriving in a rainstorm with a soggy cardboard box. What a business, a fearsome task it seems to us.

He told me that this was not a very good year for bees although the hives in his garden were doing better than the ones on the plot. I reminded him of his tale of his taking his bees on a visit to a farmer friend in another part of Kent who had ripe fields of rape. This was to "give them a holiday . . . cheer them up" he said! Whenever we see great expanses of flowering yellow we think of his bees having a "good time" on holiday!

(I wonder if the blue flax is as therapeutic? I have heard that real honey-makers scoff at the bland flavour of the rape-based honey. Certainly when the younger beekeeper gave James a pot from his own hives as a "thank you" for a favour done, we appreciated a very special taste, none of your "Blends from several countries" variety).

He said that he had done the holiday trip again this year, but evidently the bees had not shown any signs of appreciation of his solicitude.

"It's all a bit of a mystery this

beekeeping" he smiled, "but that is the part I like!"

He made his last trip up to the top of the site and paused to speak to James who, I hoped, was not asking all the same questions that I had done.

Wednesday
Delighted to discover a selfsown borage amongst the crinum lilies. It seemed very spindly, wedged between the curved shiny leaves and when I tried to remove a piece of bindweed from its soft hairy stem, pulled it out of the ground. So sadly, my joy was shortlived. I transplanted it by the tank, near the overflow for dampness but left it looking very depressed.

In the evening I read it up and found that it is an annual anyway unlike the more robust comfrey so I can only hope that someone else's plant will seed itself our way next year.

Another devotee of the blue borage flower is Lily. James caught a glimpse of her up in her garden today so I took some time off and walked up to the top of the site. Lily's garden backs onto the plots and an arch of jasmine is the only demarcation of where one finishes and the other begins. It is a beautiful garden full of interest as well as care and luckily she has found a young woman who will come in once a week and "do the heavy" for her. A rare find these days.

She offers me homemade lemonade, (which was very good) and we sit outside in the sunshine, sipping and talking. Goodness knows how we got onto bosoms but she described so well the young, awkward Lily, too well endowed for her liking, the only one in her group with bosoms, forever folding her arms across her well developed chest.

"I should have thought you would have felt proud", but the young, bashful Lily evidently thought otherwise and would have preferred to be as flat as her peers!

In such pleasant company and surroundings I spent much longer away from my plot chores than I had intended.

"You took your time" commented James but was pleased to hear that all was well with dear Lily, one of his favourite ladies.

Come to think of it, he is pretty

popular himself and a surprising number of lady plotholders come to him for "advice" or consolation!

Our alstromeria is all splayed out and straggly in spite of tieing and staking up earlier. Christopher Robin's is looking much better, a ball of gold but the roots we gave her have only been in a year so it seems that we must be much fiercer in thinning out or dividing our more mature clumps. Spring is the right time we know but maybe we should dig up all of the big clump in the autumn and discard some, that is unless anybody wants some tubers. Toby did mention that he might like some so he could risk it and heel them in, I suspect they are great survivors, certainly they are prolific.

Like Mrs Tate's ubiquitous dahlias, Auntie Elsie's alstromeria appears dotted all over our site.

Cut off the dead heads of the splendid Canterbury bells. When we were in Germany we saw some in the Kleingarten and we wondered what they were called over there, not "Canterbury" surely? "Koln" perhaps?

Evening

The newish, enthusiastic young woman was there with her own two children and a third in tow. They are all under seven I should think and to us, it seemed "way past bedtime"! They were tetchy and the air was filled with the scratching of her busy hoe and their bickering, broken frequently with cries of,

"Not there Amy, leave it . . . "

"Where's Roddy, go and find him . . . "

"Turn off that tap . . . no, right NOW!"

I found a bright jay's feather on the path and called to Amy to come and see, but immediately realised that this was not too clever an idea. The inevitable squabble was avoided only by keeping it myself for my own "collection", which was true after all, and allowing them to pick themselves a posy of marigolds.

The mother worked on. She is doing very well in fact and her corn looks good, but then she works methodically, doing a thorough clear-out, not tickling the surface here and there as some do.

The other Sunday I saw a toad sitting knee-high in the Siberian irises. I called to the children who had been running hot races up and down the main path, Amy always winning with her longer legs. They came over with their mother a little cautiously, but she said "Be careful . . . don't frighten it" so loudly that it did a U-turn and disappeared down below. The young foxes do the same, not seeming keen to be shown off before the human young ones.

The plotholder with the big yellow camper-van, topped usually with a crop of bright canoes, called out a greeting to us before he drove off. He used to teach our children swimming years ago but doesn't look a day older. Most unfair . . . I wonder what he has for breakfast?

Thursday
Miriam asked James what she should do with her flowering shallots as he roared past her in a haze of diesel oil and noise from the motor mower . . . "Chop 'em off!" he replies and was gone.

Because of Alf's hernia op' James has offered to do some of the heavier chores on the site which is typical. Too few plotholders do their share sadly and the rota for manning the shed on Sunday mornings is pretty repetitive. The first time James did his stint he got a ticking off from the ever careful Robbie who was dismayed that the receipts had been filled in in triplicate! James finding two carbons in the book assumed this was the correct procedure but evidently one was "quite enough" and the reproach of wastefulness made him feel like a naughty schoolboy! However, even Robbie has feet of clay as when the dates had to be rearranged once, he forgot that it was actually his turn and had an irate Lily phoning him to say "there was no one in the shed"!

Friday
Alf turned up to collect the shed key, roll-up in in-turned hand. We chatted in the front garden for sometime before he departed in the hard-worked little van. He seemed still worried, (as we all are), about the rumours of leases not being renewed, the takeover of the Borough.

"It's going to happen one day" he says, voicing our fears of the unpreventable, maybe inevitable.

Picked a lot of raspberries and

gooseberries in the evening and topped and tailed five pounds later, watching TV between snips. The days are delightfully long now and this is quite the best time of year when you can leave a meal in the oven to come back to, and spend some quiet time "up the plot" before the light goes entirely.

The longest day soon comes though so you must make the most of these precious hours.

Saw two foxes, or one twice.

James says that his tomato plants are too like chorus girls.

"Why chorus girls?"

"Leggy" he replies and says that he hopes they will get sturdier as they progress. They look pretty good to me, secure behind his special protective "square". This wall around them is sheets of rigid plastic held in place by a stick either side so that he can slide them along for easy watering, or deshooting. There can be quite a strong wind sometimes and this, with masses of mulching gives them a nice steamy environment usually resulting in a fair crop. Winnie has several varieties she tells us but James sticks to Moneymaker and has yet to try her favourite . . . "Gardener's Delight"!

★ ★ ★

Phil has made some splendid gooseberry and mint jelly, (our gooseberries, her mint). We called in with a lettuce for her and some raspberries and had to admire her pots cooling off on the kitchen table. It was so firm even then that it was slightly concave on top.

I have boiled mine up twice already and still have not achieved a perfect "set". The jam thermometer was right on setting point but it was too sloppy for my taste, and certainly not good enough for the Show entry. I could cheat of course and ignore the bit that says "This year's produce" and slip in a pot of mature last year's which came third! This is a nice ruby colour though so maybe I'll try just once more with some lemon juice to help.

July

GENERALLY tarted up the plot for the inspection next week probably. We are notified that certain days will be "Judgement Days" but don't know the exact ones although I suppose Alf does and Robbie.

As I was bending down finger weeding, I heard a rustle of grass on the path and a fox ambled by, stopping three yards away. I stood up but the fox didn't move, just watchful, I carried on working but keeping half an eye on him. He nosed around the raspberries and then returned past me again, sticking to the pathways making his way towards the park.

There is a new notice on the display board in the hut about foxes issued by the Borough. It tells you how to deter them with rag dipped in diesel oil, creosote, or disinfectant put down where they run regularly. They say that scraps for birds, bird tables attract them but that they scavenge as we well know. Earth worms are their main diet though so they should do well on the allotments. Sometimes they kill hedgehogs which is a pity, and rats and mice but they list their bad habits which we also know, calling and barking in the night, scattering rubbish, digging holes, (many on the plots) and leaving droppings. The last we do object to, especially on the lawn but on the whole we find their presence more a pleasure than a pain and we think that the marauding squirrels have been kept away since the fox-families moved in. Watered the onions later by holding my hand tight and flat under the tap to make a makeshift 'hose'. Hoses proper are not allowed but this handspray, used discreetly creates a useful watery arc and with skill can travel quite a long way.

Friday

Made a very late visit to the plot this evening and both saw the fox this time. He (she?) certainly is very cool, appraising us it seems and departing in its own good time, leisurely.

Kenneth, the now retired architect, two plots away from us, says he's troubled by mice eating his strawberries. Evidently they are well netted so it is not the squirrels. Have seen these pests often with the berry in their mouths making off when caught out in the act. Said he had not seen the owls much lately but this evening one was pretty vocal nearby, warming up for the nocturnal hunt.

The courgettes are forming ready for a weekend pick. They come to size very quickly and must be promptly harvested if you want them small, even daily.

Picked the last of the big lettuces, the new row looks vigorous and James sowed a new half row tonight. Sometimes I have to remind him that there are only two of us now to feed, not a family of five! Freezing some gluts is fine but there is a limit, although friends and neighbours are happy to help us out most of the time.

Picked just a handful of gooseberries, the very last I do believe. This is the third time that I have thought that! I did an adaptation of the Ambrose Heath rhubarb pudding recipe and it worked really well. I think (being greedy) that his quantities are a bit small, all right for two maybe three, but should double up if having visitors. It goes nice and crusty on top and a bit gooey underneath but you mustn't overcook it. Original recipe has a pastry shell but for health conscious gardeners it is satisfying enough without it.

Wednesday
Overcast but nicely cool. The earth is just right for a good hoeing after two nights when it rained heavily, and the soil is dark, but not too sticky. The lusty groundsel, chickweed and other rampant weeds are coming up easily for a change, roots and all.

I find it hard to call some plants weeds, like speedwell, scarlet pimpernel, buttercups, when is a wild flower a weed? Perhaps only when it restricts the thing you wish to grow and eat. Certainly ground elder has no charm for us and convolvulus likewise.

* * *

My precious marguerites have an even bigger depressed hollow in them than yesterday's and all the flowers are splayed out, almost flat. Could it be a foxy stopping place, a fight?

There is no smell though. We put a piece of chicken wire over the clump but a bit stable-doorish. I shall have to stake and tie them next visit but it looks a sad mess.

Still maintain (loyally) that foxes are mainly vegetarian but local small dog owners and cat lovers uncertain it seems.

The grocer who lives a few miles out in Green Belt country says that he kept his own free range hens, until thirty of them (he says) got beheaded or similar, fox victims. Our allotment foxes are not as wicked as this we are certain and bear no resemblance to the Beatrix Potter character. We have heard no tales of woe from the park anyway and the Canada geese could do with a cull they are saying. They prefer Croydon to Canada and are staying on for keeps states our local free newspaper!

Thursday
Mrs Somme is off to Yorkshire at the weekend so is giving her tomatoes a good watering this evening as the forecast rain has not come as promised. She asks kindly after my cough and said that she was "fine" but could do with a new pair of feet! Evidently she is much troubled by corns in spite of the NHS chiropodist's attentions. "Not like the old days" she grumbles, "then they knew you, you knew them, now it is always some one different". Being so very spare it seems odd that she would suffer from uncooperative feet, they having to bear such a little burden.

Monday
We heard from the beekeeper that the mostly cool early June has been almost a killer for bees as they do not want to come out to feed, plus the fact that they refuse to defecate in their hives. What a

terrible situation! Keepers say that this is why they are so irritable right now, understandably. However, he comforted us with the thought that these angry, hungry, constipated creatures would soon return to a more amiable state with a good bramble flowering — relief all round it seems! Told James something about a beard-swarming competition in Australia, sounds hirsute and quite terrifying I should imagine!

Mrs Tate, the dahlia lady tells us that she is allergic to bee stings and is wary of them as their plot is not far away from the hives. Concerned about their possible short tempers. Said that her nephew had had a nasty experience that week when driving on the M25. A swarm had collided with his windscreen and then a couple of bees had got inside the car through the sun roof. Luckily he was able to pull over onto the hard shoulder and get rid of them before any harm was done. Mrs Tate wins prizes with her dahlias and the tuber she gave us this year has flourished up by the herbs, spiky, pink and prolific. She says you can take them up for the winter or risk leaving them in with covering. Usually James takes them up and stores them.

Mrs Tate is a lively lady always preceding her better half as they walk up the path to their plot. He follows, less chatty but twinkling through his bifocals. "Don't know a thing about gardening" he says but seems quite happy to follow instructions as well as his wife.

Must identify sorrel or is it dock? ... think it is dock. I might make some Indian Sorrel Chutney as I now have the mint and coriander ready.

I have just been reading an article about herbs and they remind me that I should choose a dry day if I am going to do the harvesting seriously, picking the sprigs or leaves early in the morning. ("Best time to cure a bloody hangover" said Meg to a surprised Alf the other morning when he called in on the site before eight o'clock. I can think of better ways than physical exertion on an allotment but can appreciate the peace to be found there at that time).

They also said to select clean pieces so that you need not wash them at all, not bits too near the ground.

I usually make up quite small bunches, and hang them in the potting shed alongside the drying seedheads and grasses. It only takes a few weeks and then you can store them in dark glass screw-top jars and keep them out of the daylight. A new tip though is to freeze the chives and mint, not dry freeze but in cubes of ice. I haven't tried chives but made two lots of the mint. One version I chopped the fresh leaves in my food processor with a little garlic vinegar and poured the sludge into the ice-maker. The other, I just cut the leaves into small pieces and stuffed them into the cube-boxes, adding just a very little water. They rose up, in frozen green mounds but are now bagged and in the chest freezer waiting for a wintry day and a tin of "new potatoes". I have not labelled them yet and must do so or I shall be asking James yet again . . . "Do you know what this is?"!

Thinking of "new" potatoes makes me wonder if we have not lost a precious something . . . availability and technology having almost done away with truly seasonal gifts.

In the pre-freezing days the housewife adjusted her meal plans to the produce that was available at that time in her garden, plot or shops. With her apple crops, the countrywoman would have planned her orchard so that she had not only varied tastes and uses, but also a sequence of picking and storing . . . "all the year round".

There was normal ripening, natural preservation which would have pleased the "green" people! The Christmas Coxes would delight each year and the apples for the mincemeat be ready and waiting for the mincemeat mixture.

Now the seasons have been extended, overlap, for which, I am sure, we are all most grateful. But there is a price to pay and some of the real excitement has gone with the advent of this availability, except for us lucky growers, people with gardens and allotments. We can still watch the pods fatten, the tomatoes turn gold, then red, and relish the true-to-season pleasures of growing, harvesting and eating.

The depressing side to twentieth century "convenience" and marketing is that it seems that forced crops do actual damage. Water tables, erosion of the soil, even social disruption means that while we benefit, in the long term, others suffer. Maybe we all ought to campaign as we did in the war for a return to "Grow Your Own"!

This train of thought began after listening to a radio programme on asparagus growing, interviewing farmers in the Vale of Evesham.

"A mere two months season" one said, "May to June, never forced . . . Lucky if you cropped over a ton in total" . . . (Two tons to an acre).

"Not a good living, but a living".

The asparagus farmers were referred to as "grass growers" and enthused over the delights of crab tartlets or humbler ravioli as good accompaniments for their crop . . . ambrosia of the discerning gods!

The time of picked perfection was so tight that you could pick three times in a mere thirty hours it seems. It had been known for an Evensong service to be interrupted as the locals were rallied to leave the church and come to assist with yet another harvesting with the cry for assistance . . . "Come quick, the grass wants cutting again!".

★ ★ ★

In Germany last month we encountered their version of asparagus. We walked up to the Saturday street market and wandered about looking at the stalls while the children shopped for the weekend. There were many fruit and vegetable stalls, lots of flower sellers too and every couple or family seemed to be buying a bunch The produce looked good but we were puzzled by the great piles of white things, obviously seasonal and in plentiful supply. Ten or so "sticks" were bound together, like bleached carrots . . . "Spargel". Later on we ate out and ordering this found it to be a kind of asparagus but nowhere near as tasty as the English variety. The size was impressive but the flavour less so and we definitely preferred our own "grass"!

* * *

However, we did give our approval to the Teutonic version of "allotments" . . . their "Kleingarten". We visited a group of these last year and again this holiday in Essen. We walked under the old disused railway bridge out into the evening sunshine to the entrance, passing by a notice pinned to a tree trunk appealing for news of a lost rabbit. "ACHTUNG" made James and me think immediately of wartime films inevitably, for it is hard for our age group to dismiss entirely, the memories of those days even though we know that we should.

The wooden board by the allotment's entrance was ornately carved and the letters of "Gartengruppe, Sperberstrasse" twisted and turned like growing things. Once through the gate we were in another world, a world of order, profusion, tranquillity. A straight path divided the site into two halves, each plot having its own building, pathways, hedges and fences, more like a tiny village street than our own, more countryfied site. The houses were more than sheds or summer houses as we know them, rather they were mini-dwellings with curtained windows, front doors, even letter boxes!

We liked the way the crops inter-mingled so that you found pillar roses gracing an archway one side, runner beans the other . . . kohlrabbi flourishing alongside petunias . . . clematis decorating a pear tree. There was the sound of unseen water trickling somewhere and several ponds in the "gartens" sparkled by the neat green paths and lawns. We heard the bees still at work in the many foxgloves, accompanied by the

157

evensong of blackbirds and the tennis ball — thwack from humans the other side of the railway line . . . all very peaceful. It was so unlike our site and we missed the people! But we did marvel at the quality of the produce and peeped over the clipped privet to envy just a little, the excellence of the crops. The site was sheltered, low-lying, positively throbbing with life but we decided that all in all, our rougher place was better for us. These gardens were for true flat-dwellers and replaced the garden they could not have; into this situation, they grew their produce and very well too. These were fulfilled dreams, with green plums and pears, blue delphiniums, pink pinks, even a German gnome, all showing much loving care and substitution on a high level, I don't think the weeds would dare to grow there!

The eschscholzia had closed for the night and the flowers reminded us of our German neighbour plotholder back home. We noticed that there was a mixture of colours, not just golds but some soft pinkish-brown ones too. We get teased about our "Mexican Hogweed" which is, in fact a more innocent angelica but in the Kleingarten there were several great clumps of the dread plant surprisingly, magnificent in the setting sun with its sculptural leaves but a danger!

We noticed a new kind (to us) of plant supports, a kind of corkscrew of metal staking up efficiently the rows of tomato plants, "Good for broad beans" said James.

* * *

Later that same trip we went over into Holland and there found a site much more like ours. It covered a large area beside a canal, a broad flat sweep of land crisscrossed with pathways and plots. Patches of colour showed where the flowers were, much like the commercial rectangles we had seen on a much larger scale that visit. As we walked home after our evening meal we saw many people still at work in the fading light, one or two sweeping their watering cans into the convenient water of the canal, no threat of bans or standpipes there!

Friday pm

A handsome hot young runner comes panting into the car park, a bit lost it seems. He has a tiny map on a scrap of paper in his hand obviously confusing him. We are able to point him in the right direction but wonder if he will get through the park before it closes as it is nearly 9 o'clock. Maybe he does have time as the thick clouds coming up make it darker than usual and we hadn't heard the keeper's warning whistles yet. In years gone by it wasn't whistles but a single bell, a great clanger that sounded right across the park. The replacements sound peevish compared with the louder, more mellow, sounding brass.

"Bells" said Coleridge "are the poor man's only music". I am not at all sure I agree with him but I suppose he meant church bells as opposed to the concert hall. What about birdsong, water, just plain singing? Nowadays you get it thrust upon you unsolicited and irritating in the form of unwanted Muzak.

★ ★ ★

160

James got the mower from the shed up the top and did a push and shove job after I had done the path edges. It all looks pretty organised now, plenty of produce, good courgettes and lettuces, you can almost see them grow! The courgettes that hide and become marrows are still cookable and their skins are not tough, you can eat the lot.

* * *

As we left an owl flew from the beech trees and disappeared into the park silently. The last to leave I waited by the gate while James drove out but didn't stay to shut it as intended. Reason . . . the sight of a stag beetle. I cannot stand them and fled to the car in the road leaving him to lock up.

Saturday
At home . . . Saw a bullfinch on the nut feeder and later the spotted woodpecker. He left a striped feather behind on the grass but I put it on the kitchen window sill outside and it blew away. I have quite a collection of pretty feathers now, the

gifts of our parakeets mostly, slim spears of chrome yellow, brilliant green or turquoise. Some are shorter, dark grading to green and these, with the occasional smaller jay's feather. They get put into a little wooden "vase" that Sarah gave me, (ostensibly for grasses I believe, but ideal for feathers in fact). I shall need another similar one soon I fear, as the neck of this one is packed jam-tight now.

Sunday
What universal music a recorder makes. We heard someone practising while we strolled back from that meal in Holland a few weeks ago, now we are greeted on our morning arrival at the allotments with a similar sound. It was very pleasing at first, (this alfresco home concert), accompanying our weeding, but became a little disconcerting as it progressed into a selection of Christmas carols! In July? In the hot eighties?

"Once in Royal David's City" . . . "Silent Night" . . .

"Feels like Australia" remarked Christopher Robin "all this sun and carols!"

Her helper offered us some of his radishes. "The wife likes them, I don't" he told us and we were the lucky ones with a great bunch of the red variety, plus a single huge white one which he said she usually stir-fried together with other vegetables.

Monday
Last tidy up before a brief time away. It turned out that James had borrowed "my" secateurs yesterday and left them on the path by the raspberries all night. Some kind person however had hung them up by the strap on a stake so much relieved. I am glad not to have lost them as they not only serve as an efficient pruner and trimmer but remind me of their giver. Too far away in distant Yorkshire lives the other daughter battling with job and family and an often inhospitable climate. Gardening is in her blood though and many a phonecall from us has to be postponed as she is out squeezing the last drop of faint daylight for a bit of work, after work. The children's bathtime may be missed and the chance to have a quiet,

wind-down cigarette, (like her maternal grandfather) makes its claim, but she battles away with sour black soil, empty cans from the student's digs, frolicking dog and small, if beloved, feet. She wins though and within the windblown sounds of cricket and Rugby crowds, raises a garden that looks cherished and really tries to please!

Nina has complained yet again (to Alf) of "doggy poo" on her plot . . . "Great dollops" she moans. It is in our lease that dogs are only allowed on the site if on a leash. Alf puts his reminders up underlined in red but apparently all to no avail. Maybe we need a more explicit poster, graphically illustrated and even more underlining!

I wonder why some particular weeds, (wild flowers) seem to flourish beside particular crops? I noticed again today that there is a lot of scarlet pimpernel around the garlic and shallots. Then there are patches of blue speedwell, so pretty too, alongside the runner bean-plants. Of course there is chickweed everywhere and groundsel but only a few pieces of ground elder appear now,

164

we really seem to have rid ourselves of it over the years.

Last week I noticed some blackfly beginning to coat the green stems of the marguerite clump up by the herb garden.

I remembered reading somewhere that marigolds planted near some crops kept pests away so I decided to try and transplant a couple although they were in full flower. Maybe this would disperse the fly before the buds opened.

I carried them up with plenty of soil on their roots and began to dig a deep hole for them by the marguerite clump. I became aware of a kind of muffled roar, unfocussed, but I could see no mowers and the car park looked peaceful. I turned my head to look up the top plots and saw a great cloud, a swirling mass of bees supposedly! I threw my trowel down and walked, not quite running, to the car park. After a few minutes I saw that Meg was up there still, apparently not too concerned so I went back skirting the plot where the bees were and joined her. Over near the flats some workmen were making quite a din with a digger and Meg said that probably this racket was disturbing them, hence their indeterminate whizzing about. She said too that they had been restless the day before, looking for a new home obviously. I returned to my planting and about an hour later walked up with the younger beekeeper to see if anything had happened. By this time two clumps of pulsating bees had formed at either end of a raspberry support, mixed up with the canes, thick brown ropes. "Two virgins probably" he said allowing a bee to crawl up his uncovered arm.

"They aren't aggressive now" he reassured us, letting it be, "They are only defensive when they have a home to defend and right now they are homeless".

He was more concerned about the problems caused by their choice of twiggy and leafy support. It was so much easier if they swarmed on a branch of a tree then, he said, you could lop it off above them and catch the swarm in a box.

"They're not ours" he told us (how did he know?) but for general safety's sake wanted a collection. Evidently the bee scouts would be out now looking for a suitable home or homes and once this was found would return with the message and off they would go.

I walked up later and saw just the one mass but bigger . . . then on the next visit, about an hour later found them all gone, not a bee in sight! I hope they found a place safe for them, safe from the human point of view too.

Sunday
A new face turned out to be a temporary "helper".

"Just come to give Tom a hand" she said, having asked me the right route for the shared compost heap area. She stopped on her return journey to admire the delphiniums, so tall so blue in the sunshine. Sadly all her own plants had been devoured by slugs at the tender stage. She said that she found us all much friendlier on this site, "nicer than Dulwich" But she added that she liked her own plot there, and was resisting her friend's pleas to desert Dulwich and join us and him, to share his plot. I gathered that they were just "good friends" so maybe their separate allotment space is a wise thing for now. She looked down at her small grubby hands ruefully.

"Just look at these . . . Goodness knows what my tutor will say tomorrow . . . I'm on a massage course!"

But we both agreed that although gardening gloves are really needed most of the time, it is the actual earth-touch that satisfies. Sometimes the warmth of the soil comes as a surprise and the feel of it on your actual skin is sensuous and close. Having said this, my own hands are pretty disgusting and the roughness of the right one good enough for sandpapering wood!

Tuesday
Three people have now asked us for some of our Peruvian lilies. We have looked them up to find that they are Alstroemerias. So far they have been "Auntie Elsie's lilies" as like so many of our plants they have associations with people, friends or relatives. We think that these on the plot are "Lutea", bright deep yellow with carmine markings. Anyway it must be about three years now since we

planted them on the plot and this is the first summer that they have bloomed really well. We thought that we should be dividing them up in the autumn but the book says separate the tubers in March, or early April and to keep as much of the original soil as possible when planting out. Heather's partner plotholder said that she had bought some quite expensive seed at the Chelsea Flower Show last year but had had no success whatsoever. They do look attractive and last for such a long time when picked. One of their admirers said he called them "station" flowers as they were very much in evidence for sale to commuters at the Junction each evening.

★ ★ ★

So many of our plants and shrubs have "belonging" names. Our prospective daughter-in-law was amused at this strange family that seemed to have christened not only most of the things growing in the garden but also items of furniture too . . . Uncle Kenneth's desk; Great Aunt Nan's mirror . . . outside,

Minna's hydrangea; Edith's hellebore; Miss Robert's myrtle bush . . . and so on. Now she is one of us and does likewise we notice and like us is saddened by any loss. Minna's hydrangea was nearly killed off one dry summer but when we dug the stump up we found two green shoots, small but apparently healthy. With great care we separated these and replanted them about a foot apart, mulching the ground really well first. They appear to have survived so far and we shall just have to be patient and wait and see. It is a perfectly pure white one and came from Minna's cottage garden in Guestling. She had been up to the village church one day where there had been a recent funeral. The flowers were still on the grave, I don't remember whose, and she broke off a small piece of the pure white hydrangea. This must have been well over fifty years ago I should think, when she planted it by her cottage front door, to strike and bloom for her, then us, so we do not want to lose it. It never shows a whisper of pink or blue but has absolutely white full blooms after the pale cream buds.

I suppose you could replace it with one from a garden centre but it wouldn't be the same.

★ ★ ★

Minna was a lovely person, living a long life, ninety-four years, most of these in the same part of Sussex, but she the least narrow of persons, broad-minded, understanding, forthright and kindly. She looked after "Missie", our great aunt, her companion and protector, and was as realistic and practical as Auntie was erratic in spite of her nursing background — (Queen's nurse with service medals in a gilt frame to prove it, and the wars in our history books were real memories for her). Their cottage was one of a pair and typically Auntie had sliced off their garden so that they had the lion's share, leading down to an overgrown orchard. Yet another piece of land was hers, up the lane, and here were fruit trees with two fringed, much mended hammocks and a rickety summer house for our use when we visited. It was a place of damp grass, bees' hum, butterflies, perpetual sunshine as the dappling from the leaves patterned our closed eyelids as we swung gently from side to side, ignoring calls to "come on in".

For overflow visitors there was a hut at the bottom of the cottage garden named "Uncle Tom's cabin", (more names!). We all longed to be allowed to sleep there but I did so only once, being the youngest and therefore the least trustworthy.

It had a single iron bedstead in it, a chest of drawers with a mottled mirror and runner on top. There were sepia photos of Auntie "at War", her huge nurse's headress almost as big and stiff as a Breton nun's. The wan young, so young men around her smile the asked-for smile, the horrors shelved for that moment. A brown print of "The Angelus" was on one wall and over the bed was a reindeer's horn, engraved with jolly tiny figures but the leather cover concealed a rusty but short sharp knife, probably for skinning game. The cottage too was full of things from foreign places, an Aladdin's cave for us children. Uncle Tom's smelled of damp and camphor and was inhabited by woodlice and spiders. Luckily the slugs stayed outside! The path leading down to it was a dangerous collection of uneven stones but flanked by flowers spilling over from the tiny lawn. Missie had bought some trees from Woolworths many many years earlier which had turned out to be far from "dwarf" and reared in a great dark green wall all down one side of the garden, dripping and moaning in the squally wind from the sea. On a fine day you could see a minute triangle of sea over to the left of Fairlight church but only from one of the cottage bedroom windows. When it rained the most enormous slugs crawled up the outside walls and the little house became chill until the fire was lit, the paraffin lamps lighting us to bed too early it always seemed. The creaking wooden floor of my bedroom usually shared with parent or sisters, was also the ceiling of the sitting room and I remember as the youngest one, banished to bed first, and much too soon I thought, posting little notes of complaint through the cracks in the floor. Through slivers of downstairs light which let through just a murmer of grown-up talk, my paper protest would float down into the room to be ignored!

Minna was tiny, rosy cheeked, dark hair back in a tight bun always and her eyes were bright behind her tinted glasses. When she gardened she bent straight over from the waist so that she was halved. "Now are you sure you are not taking on too much?" she would say, perceptive and concerned. There was no deceiving Minna. And how she remembered things, little details about the children, events past, things to come, maybe it was this outside herself attitude that kept her so young in heart. When she died she left a little gift of money to each of us sisters and our children. I bought a piece of agate with mine, a smooth swirl of coloured rings with a tiny piece of bright green deep in its centre.

Thursday pm
Fine and cool. Did a really good double act of my hand weeding up the rows of beetroot while James followed with the hoe. He dug up a sample potato plant and was pleased to find ten clean white spuds. Should be a good crop if typical.

It seemed particularly quiet this evening, virtually no birdsong except for a bit of robin trill. No geese-noise or quacking from the park either but it must have been a Cub's night out there as there was a lot of human whoops and shrieks in the woods. Probably the reason for no fox visit this time, decidedly not their kind of cub.

The house reeked of ratatouille all day after a great session with courgettes, mushrooms et al. Added a can of tomatoes and some finely chopped garlic. Freezing some and eating the rest.

Sunday
Spider — Tiny thumbnail brown one on the beetroots. Finger weeding at the time so focussed on him (or her). Brilliant scarlet spots on the legs but not the body — curious.

★ ★ ★

First prize again for the best allotment site in Kent! We hope that the departed Hon. Sec. Mrs Wilsher will be celebrating in that great allotment in the sky! She did worry so, working hard to achieve good results. We will remember another, less successful year when we were confronted in the car park with a large board propped up by the gate for all to see.

The rain had seeped under the plastic covering and the red felt tipped reproach shed pink tears. "County Allotment Competition results. We came only third. Rather disappointing. My thanks to those who made the effort, for those who did not, enough said." She would hint or nag according to ones just deserts it seemed, making no allowances for poor health, family commitments, pressures of work. You had to admire her very real dedication to the site but on occasions we would do a crossed fingers witch sign if we saw her approaching, ready to defend our shaggy edges, unmown paths, crop of splendid weeds. Alf, our present Hon. Sec, has an altogether more relaxed approach but even he heaves the occasional despairing sigh as someone does something stupid with their weeds, or piles the uncombustible bits on the bonfire heap, the worst act of this kind being the depositing of a Gaz can, hopefully empty, on the combustible pile!

"Idiots!" says Alf with justification.

When "Kent" were due to come the following week Alf organised a working party for the preceding Saturday and Sunday. A plea for volunteers went up but were thin on the ground sadly. It then turned out that Alf had to go off somewhere so James was asked to supervise the helpers for the Saturday, clearing the top area by the park where Alf planned to reclaim four disused plots and make a kind of glade eventually. We had the names of the volunteers, (all three of them) and as we passed a seated figure on Percy's plot, called out "Are you Mr Robinson?" He was not so we went up to the top armed with our pitchforks and rakes in the blazing sun. It would have to be the hottest day of this summer!

We soon became a sweaty band of three working away to rake off the grass left by Alf's strimmer but it was only an hour later that the first man wandered up to say that he was a "helper" in fact, changed from the Sunday list to Saturday due to an "unforseen commitment" and had not realised we were the actual working party! Poor communication all round as although not Mr Robinson, was a "worker"! Not that he did much but spent a lot of time brow-mopping and sighing. When Mr Robinson did turn up, with apologies for being late, he did a grand job and the dry leftover grasses and brambles soon became a great pile ready for burning. I picked up twigs and branches from the trimmed or fallen trees and added these to the pile until I could no longer reach the top.

There were still a lot of brambles and bricks around and great hollows so you had to watch your step all the time. I took my turn with the pitchfork and dragged up the dry dusty hay, feeling sweaty and Thomas Hardy'ish but lacking the statutory flagon of cider! We all could have done with this but had to make do with warm lemonade, sitting in the welcome shade of the beech tree and sycamores that would encircle our "glade" if we ever achieve it. It looked a long way off at present.

We stopped altogether after a few hours as the heat really was intense and we said that we might return in the cooler evening. ("maybe not" I said).

We left it looking a little more civilised and with two piles of rubbish ready to burn when Alf was back and it wasn't too dry.

The foxes are not too happy about all these goings-on as they have their runs up there but if they decide to shift further back into the actual wild part of the adjacent park we would not be too sorry. They are a very mixed blessing really and it is a great pity that people feed them.

★ ★ ★

Did in fact return in the evening and saw that someone else had done some further work up there. A kind person who had heard me remark on a clump of borage had rescued a big piece and left in a half-filled watering can by our tool box. How thoughtful. I shall plant it tomorrow and hope it revives after its move. We left the clearing with its two bonfire piles golden in the setting sun, looking like a couple of Monet hayricks.

Sunday
More tidying work for the visitation. This time the rubbish area. Worked with Winnie clearing out the accumulated rubbish in the bins and boxes, not a pleasant job! Puddles of revolting slime lined the plastic and wooden containers

with populations of soggy snails, some alive, some definitely dead. We were both glad of our rubber gloves. There is always a lot of broken glass around due to the old greenhouses we imagine. You are forever picking pieces out of the earth if you have a plot in a certain area and this applies to our top one.

It seems strange that people don't take their rubbish home, like containers of slug pellets, cracked flower pots, plastic seed trays. Someone has to deal with them and surely they have their own domestic refuse collection?

There is a large white-painted notice by the area which clearly says "SITE RUBBISH ONLY" . . .

"Silly buggers can't read!"

Tuesday
Lots of weeds again and side shoots keep growing on the tomatoes as fast as you pick them out, they seem to appear overnight! Only wildlife or similar seen today was a black and white cat scuttling by into the park.

★ ★ ★

James commented tonight on a large silver jet flying low on the flight path over the allotments, describing it as "impossible". I know what he means. Concorde is even more amazing, I don't know why some people call it a "death's head" more like an elegant moth or a great fish, functional but beautiful too.

It has its own special roar as it sweeps round in a great curve over the site on its regular route. It commands attention and we straighten ourselves gazing upwards. Aeroplanes often criss-cross the site, low; high, out of sight in clouds; little horse-fly buzzers, red winged; watchful police helicopters out to spot a burglary, molestation in the park; they all are part of the scene the only exception being a rare earsplitting visit by a fighter when they have some event over at Biggin Hill.

We both remember well the sky battles in the last war, the dog-fights of the Battle of Britain. On the way to and from school we would look up at the white squirls, the planes almost too high to be seen, specks at the most. Somehow we never associated these with the still warm metal pieces we picked up from the pavements and road. The guns and the enemy at that time were noises and abstraction, not yet flesh and blood. "War" was disturbed nights, sleeping in the cellar, lessons in the shelter and a whole chain of teachers — comings and goings punctuated by gas mask practices, rubbery giggles and steamed up visors, and knitting things for an adopted Merchant Navy ship with wool smelling of creosote. I wonder what those sailors thought of their parcels? In return they sent us a big painting of their ship tossing about on a splendid green sea. We "Dug for Victory" dutifully in the school garden, each with a little plot but I cannot recall any actual produce so maybe my green fingers had not yet developed.

Reality came with Pathe news in the local cinema; skeletal figures barely alive in striped pyjamas; flame-throwers in the jungle, figures burning alive.

Friday
My transplanted marigolds (the day of the swarming) have taken after all and

almost at once the columns of blackfly on the marguerite stems have vanished. Maybe a coincidence but I prefer to think that my "green" solution to the problem actually worked.

Alf told James that our double plot has been entered for the Dexter cup this year, a Borough award for a larger plot . . . What a compliment! We are very pleased as although we know that we shall be way down the list in points, ("Marks for good husbandry, planning and produce accrued" etc.) we represent our site among the total of eleven and shall be entitled to attend the bunfight later in the month or early August.

The County judges have come and gone but there will soon be the visitation of the local group so all those plotholders with their pink tickets displayed will be paying every attention to their "presentation"!

Hope it will be on a fine day for like a suburban high street, a little bit of sunshine can do wonders to the total effect.

Tuesday
Late evening. There have been ominous
rumbles of thunder today and a great
build-up of slatey clouds. Mrs Somme
is just back from a walking holiday in
Scotland and although someone in her
absence has done some desultory weeding
for her it all looks a bit shaggy.

After she had gone off on her bicycle
we found two plastic bottles bobbing
about in the lower water tank, leftovers
from her own special watering method.
The aftermath is sometimes piles of
greening plastic containers but these can
be tolerated. We do not know her actual
age but suspect that she must be in her
eighties.

Thursday
Did not have a chance to get up to the
plot during the day. Now the breeze
was dropping, the sounds of bells clear
being Tuesday, practise night, at Saint
George's. For the whole time we were
there they rang. At 9 o'clock they stopped
but after a pause launched into another
peal. Maybe they needed a breather, or
an admonition, correction, call of nature?

At 9.20 a single note is repeated but even this is not the end as yet another peal sounds before the final silence.

There is still quite a bit of birdsong which will lessen when August comes, but this evening there are thrushes, robins, blackbirds, wood pigeons, crows and others all settling down for the night.

★ ★ ★

I remarked to Kenneth as he passed by that the sparrow hawks seemed very vocal tonight and he agreed but said that they were, in fact, kestrels. I found this interesting because I had called them this way back to Robbie and he (all-knowing), said I was wrong, they were sparrow hawks. I stood corrected but evidently I was right the first time, as Kenneth observes them with binoculars from his town house window and sees their markings quite clearly. I felt a slight sense of triumph because Robbie does rather tend to lay down the law! He is a great winner of prizes and cups at the allotment show and sure enough again this year he will carry off the trophy for the best plot in the Borough! We walked up there the other evening and thought that it looked good but not spectacular, preferring the less regimented plot that Winnie has up our "East End".

Here, things seem to flourish happily whereas there, (the West End) they thrive under duress.

You have to admire Robbie though for when he had a broken leg he was still working away up there, balancing dangerously with one crutch, determined not to let things get out of hand.

His great boast was that one Sunday lunch they had seven vegetables from the plot. Now we count ours, "better than Robbie" we say, or, "not so good" unless that is, you are allowed to count parsley, or mint, as proper "produce"!

Saturday
Tied up the tomatoes for the third time. The big sucker that James had pulled up roots and all then replanted, has taken so this too got its support to give it encouragement, an act of faith.

Didn't check the bean crop this visit as the rumblings seemed to be getting nearer and more frequent so helped James pick fruit in case the heavens opened. Noticed that one of the sunflowers had its leaves twirling about, quite fiercely, although they are sheltered by the trees and there was no breeze, a sort of storm presage, a Tournesol barometer? Indeed, huge spots of rain did begin to fall soon after and we got to the car only just in time. Didn't wait for it to pass but went home directly and ate two huge bowls (one each), of raspberries, redcurrants and cream!

Friday

Going away for the weekend so made an early morning call, unusual time for us. The sun seemed in the wrong place! Picked masses of beans and peas, lettuces too. My earlier criticism of limpness is now unfounded as these are much crisper and hearty. Maybe it is just when they are cloched up that they seem more leathery.

Tuesday

Went up to water. At least the weeds too are dry and dusty and not growing either. Still having to watch out for side-shoots on the tomatoes. Found a whopper that we had missed. What a lovely smell bruised tomato leaves have.

Watered the carrots and beetroots but wondered if they will swell up at all with this lack of real rain. The courgettes have had another spurt and I picked ten nice-sized ones. I wish we had some 'real' marrows though as well as I do like them stuffed or with white sauce.

The gourds are looking more interesting, some about teacup size. I wonder what their limit is? Phil had a dish of spectacular ones, dried and varnished, really beautiful as a decoration.

We have two enormous pumpkins growing well. Someone gave James the seeds and challenged him to a private competition.

★ ★ ★

When Jack was small the other Jack, the plumber plotholder, showed him how to "blow up" a marrow by feeding it a rich sugar solution. A piece of darning wool was sewn into the stem of a young marrow and the trailing end of the wool placed in a saucer of the solution. An efficient capillary action fed the marrow more nourishment than it needed, so enlarging it to splendid mammoth proportions. He also told Jack to carve his initials into the skin of the marrow when he began the exercise so that he could watch them grow too. It worked!

I picked the new spinach and we had some for supper with a couple of eggs and a bit of streaky. It was so fresh and needed hardly any cooking, just steaming.

Saturday
Still a lot of watering needed. We are lucky to have a tank at each end of the plots and as you water, you leave the tap on to replace the canfuls taken. It chivvies you on as it refills so that you have a race to beat the overflow hole, and work all the faster! The top tank, a smaller square one has nice clean water but the lower one, bath-size, is a bit murky at present.

Maybe it is in need of a scoop to get out some of the accumulated sludge.

Nasty smelly job which tends to get put off to yet another day.

Mrs Somme once had some watercress growing by our lower tank. It did quite well but we didn't repeat the kindness as we planned to clear around the area and concentrate on courgettes and lettuces the following year. Had a chat with the ex publican and his wife just back from Majorca. ("Only 82 degrees there") Seemed to be glad to be back on their plot and home again.

Monday
Went up on my own this evening and could not resist picking a few loganberries from next door's plot, one up, as they were dropping off, so I took just a few for a fruit salad, such lovely rich coloured juices.

Must have left the hoe there on Saturday but hadn't realised it. Glad to find it laid out on our box by some good neighbour. As I padlocked the gate I felt something on my head, not the terror of a June-bug surely, maybe a bird dropping? But suddenly the heavens opened with a terrific unexpected hailstorm! I sheltered under the trees as there seemed to be no lightning or thunder around. It felt good to be both cool and damp for a change, (Lady Chatterley but no Mellors sadly).

A little boy who had been playing outside the town houses on his bike was called in by his mother. He flung his bike into the open garage but delayed going in, skipping about the drive with his arms flung out, shouting with delight, his face upturned blinking with the great cool drops.

The Hon. Sec. very kindly gave me a lift home in his car. I made his seat wet and apologised. Sadly the rain stopped as suddenly as it had started and left only a surface damp. We could do with a lot more.

Thursday
Asked Percy's advice about our corn crop. James thought that he had heard somewhere that you should take off the lower sideshoots once the plants were full height. ("elephant's eye"!) . . . did Percy know?

He said that he had never grown

sweetcorn himself but in the fields, nobody bothered to surely? True, so we decided to leave them, soaking up the sunshine and the water.

The pressure on the upper tank is very low at the moment so there is no chance of using our flattened hand ploy. All the world and his wife must be using water right now. God preserve us from another year of standpipes!

James used to call the man on the plot near us the "rainmaker" as he always seemed to bring it with him but we could do with his talents now!

Saturday
Prayers answered.

Caught in a rainstorm too heavy to be ignored. Sheltered under the sycamore trees on the top plot. The forecast had got it right for once but we had hoped to cut the grass and do the edges and if time, some leek planting too but had to give up and beat a retreat.

The newest plotholder, the Wyf of Bath joined us, with her gap-toothed smile and nice ample proportions. She had been up to the communal compost heap to rid herself of her load of weeds but had too far to go to her car with the empty wheelbarrow, not in this deluge anyway. Her T-shirt was already darkened with rain but she decided after a few minutes to "make a dash for it" and charged down the pathway, bosoms a wobble under the bright Mexican motif.

James had been caught in the middle of planting out some leeks and had got a really wet back already, and soon we realised that we were not being protected by the trees at all, but rather wettened still further by the accumulated drips on the covering leaves. We opted to ignore the rain and have faith in a bit of "Dutchman's" trousers in the East. It did in fact soon widen and we returned to our labours, steaming with the earth!

★ ★ ★

At home the almost empty water butt was half full, just in one day!

Cooked for the very first time courgette flowers, dipping them in batter then frying them lightly. They were quite nice, certainly decorative. Christopher Robin's friend who had lived in Italy said that they had often had courgette flowers in omelettes. I wonder if these were sweet or savoury?

★ ★ ★

In the evening a bright yellow (zeppelin-style) balloon flew over the house, its engine chugging away, advertising Classic FM. At the time we were being forced to endure, not enjoy, the bellowing of "live" music from pub in the high street. We are all for live entertainment, participation, but wondered how the actual audience-by-choice could tolerate all those decibels. If we, quite a distance away, could hear it all too well, those nearer must surely have been deafened! There was a lot of electric guitaring and sixties pop songs, classics of their kind (and well remembered by us) but it was a real racket which we added to by cutting our front lawn with the electric mower, but even then could hear the "music" above the whine.

Tuesday
Saw the fox heralded by a short bark. The man with the white shaggy dog appeared from the top plots and the dog on his lead began to bark too. The fox walked down to the tank end and stood looking at me before doing a U-turn over our plot going back over its tracks. The dog was going mad all the while.

Lovely evening, cloudless and orange-pink.

Mrs Somme made us offerings from her good things, early beans and fine spinach, swapped talk about garlic growth, "comes up from nowhere" she says. Scattered two sacks of grass cuttings (from the neighbours; who is doing who a kindness?)

Swifts flying low for midges.

Practise night at the Parish. At the end of the session they seemed to go berserk, all ringing their bells in joyous disorder, a real jam session. You have a mental picture of ribald ringers up-and-downing, clinging to their ropes in irreverent bobbing. It reminded us of a certain wedding peal at a family wedding when the elderly verger, unsteadily balanced on one narrow foot, had the other foot caught, (intentionally), in a looped rope for bell number two. Pumping up and down he rang the double peal with great verve and skinny bony hands, a frail grinning figure celebrating the happy couple's troth in the tiny village church by the stream.

Wednesday
Collected the watering can from the box and walked up the path to the tomato patch. The fox was walking towards us looking as if he had been expecting this visit. He changed his mind though and turned quietly to retrace his steps. We finished the watering and James fetched the mower to cut the paths. Again he was met by the fox by the shed showing no fear at all, possibly expecting some titbit? And again, when only a few feet away, turned and went off across the freshly sown carrots, but delicately. Usually they keep to the paths. No barking today just a very dignified exit.

Not a cloud in the sky, very warm, a real old-fashioned summer's evening.

★ ★ ★

A notice has gone up announcing a change of date for the allotments party. We shall be away for the new date which is a pity. Bert had asked around the plots who would be interested in a party and although we had agreed that it was a nice idea we were not too sure about having it in the church hall. This smacked of formality a little and taking us out of the environment where we all knew each other. You do not always immediately recognise a plotholder out of his gardening clothes, on a train, in an office, sharing a pew, when we wear different "hats". Years ago someone organised a splendid evening barbecue, at Halloween I think it was . . . all burned sausages and moths in the candlelight. The hut was decorated, music played, punch flowed and a noisy good time was had by all, still keeping their outdoor plot identity. The neighbours did not mind as for the most part they were there in person, enjoying themselves too.

If given a choice and if these other arrangements fail to collect enough supporters, we thought we might tentatively suggest a repeat performance, but tactfully.

August

IT may be a bit harder work getting your plots up to scratch for the local inspection but if your site enters them for an "award", a cup, then you will reap a reward in receiving a smart invitation card for Presentation Evening! (with guest). We were surprised but obviously pleased to be entered for a cup awarded to a plotholder with over 6 rods to manage. We knew that we stood no chance against the "experts" but had achieved some kind of standard. Winnie quite rightly, was one of the nominees in a different category, Meg too, and for the first time Miss Tear, or rather Miriam really. Miriam doesn't like functions so we were unable to persuade her to come but Percy had been invited as someone else's guest, so in the end we all met on the day at the Civic Hall, looking almost unrecognisable in our clean clothes!

Robbie was there, (with "her indoors" as he calls his devoted wife, we imagine forever slaving over a hot stove preparing all those vegetables); he in his capacity as a hard working chief secretary of all the sites, the whole local society . . . an unenviable task. Who could or will replace him?

The evening was fine and we all gathered into allotmenty groups with our sherries or juices before going inside for the presentations. Seated on hard chairs in formal rows we watch and applaud as familiar names are read out, favoured sites, dedicated gardeners. One award goes to a plotholder under the age of 35 and a pretty girl gets a wolf whistle as she returns smiling to her seat. One of "us" gets a cup and in his absence Alf goes up so we all give him a hearty cheer. The whole process takes an extra long time as the local paper's photographer insists on popping up onto the platform at every award, (3rd; 2nd; joint 1sts and so on) which takes an age as the giver and receiver clasp hands and turn to smile at the flash.

The Deputy Mayor does his stuff about "Leisure" and then we have a slide show. The slides are of the sites and plots and some get muddled up, and there are jovial loud comments over the speaker who has got it wrong. By then we are all waiting to hear which site has won the most points overall. Ours has often been first but again, this year, we are second to Abbeyfield, ("Lost points on paths" says Alf but with no reproach. We had all done our best and can hardly compete with a site that can afford paving!)

Later we learn that the same order has applied to the County awards so we have to be content with another second this year and feel like taking a sneaky look at our rivals to see what edge they really have on us. We can dismiss local judges but not County ones so readily!

The buffet is ready for our attention now and the talking over for another year. We home in to our friendly tables and consume sandwiches and quiche over wine and beer just pleased to be in good company.

Winnie's guest asks if she can have our Tandoori chicken drumstick bones, "for my foxes". Evidently she has seven who regularly appear at the bottom of her garden at 6 o'clock and have been known to return for "seconds" We wrap them in our blue paper napkins and hand them over. We liked the image of this line of foxes queueing up like school dinnertime. She admitted that when she found that there were no suitable scraps she made sandwiches, ("Brown bread of course" we said), filling them with dog food. At least she gives them a sensible diet not like someone we know who gives them chocolate bars . . . silly man.

★ ★ ★

Miss Tear was all excited about her bat boxes and told me all the saga as we ate our tuna (not Pal), sandwiches. She has a gadget that detects bat-calls and had persuaded the local authority to put up some boxes in the park opposite her town house. We hope the bats prove their existence and come there to roost. We have seen them sometimes, swooping over the plots at dusk but are not often there ourselves so late. She was shocked by a remark of one of the park people organising the fixing of her boxes, regarding a sick-looking tree.

"Needs watering probably" he said "but we only get paid for certain things and watering's not one of them".

Upset by this attitude and the sickly tree she and Miriam carted buckets of water over into the park and gave the tree some drink, typically thoughtful. A lady councillor comes to chat and we lay it on thick how necessary allotmenteering is for health and sanity. She agrees of course and we pray for more years granted to our current lease. Alf tells her of a new need, that is for smaller plots, not even 5 but $2\frac{1}{2}$, for people who are a bit frail but long for some soil in their flat-dwelling lives, somewhere to be with real things, a little patch. So he advocates plot-sharing at our site and it seems to be working. There is nothing much worse than having too much ground to care for and getting all steamed up over "being behind" as we know well!

When it seems time to go and the attendants are beginning to clear the coffee cups away briskly, we make our way to the car park in the rain and like true gardeners, sniff the damp air and welcome it . . . a very pleasant occasion over for another year.

Monday
Afternoon visit. Christopher Robin had been there most of the day. She said she had got a bad splinter in her hand and had to find Tom with his Swiss Army knife equipped with tweezers to remove it. She was pleased when I told her where to get one of these, as "son-in-laws were always a problem when it came to birthdays". We both picked our fruit, raspberries and loganberries, talking, not always listening. As I went out of earshot I would make friendly noises until back near her again. Usually we are all pretty quiet with just the occasional remark one to another, but today seemed to be a talking day and we both agreed that it was pleasant to have a bit of company for what is after all, a pretty boring job after the first row done.

★ ★ ★

Found some enormous gooseberries near the ground, almost golden and ready to burst. I do not remember them ever being so huge before.

Wednesday
Both decided that "some plot" would be therapeutic. Grey skies though and it began to rain quite hard in little bursts, but we stuck it out to finish our "programme". It was very quiet, only pigeons and one robin to listen to and only four people around. Grubbed up the mass of chickweed and other stuff so that James could plant some more leeks. Yesterday's double row looked a trifle limp so he watered them again although the earth is still blackish-brown with rain. Puddled in new rows today, now SEVEN in all! But we like leeks!

Friday pm
Saw Toby and asked if Henni was all right as we had not seen her for a while. Evidently it is just a question of not being up there at the same time and she is fine.

Last time we talked together she was telling me about a recipe for soft fruits with a name so German I could not keep it in my head! I said that there was a similar one, using cornflour too that I had which was Danish, (with an equally unpronounceable name). When she lived as a child in Stuttgart, fruit country, she had enjoyed this dessert, but my recollection is of rather a powdery taste. Anyway, I am into sorbets at present so shall probably keep to these. I don't know how the conversation got onto corsets but I think it was to do with being energetic on the plot, and the fact that it gave you a good appetite so output input tended to cancel each other out. "You never wear a belt" exclaimed the shocked saleslady to Henni when she tried on a skirt recently. We found that neither of us did these middle-aged days, unless a really formal occasion demanded it and then only were we prepared to suffer for appearances sake. Our girlish shape had changed, not for the better alas, but we preferred freedom now, to be "unfettered". Anyway, where does it actually go, it must go somewhere? Henni loves the allotments, "everyone here is so nice" she says, "plot people are such nice people" and I think she is right, for the most part anyway. But there was one woman some time ago who was a terrible Jeremiah, everything was always wrong, nothing right. Every disaster that could strike did strike, every pest that nibbled, nibbled her crops, every seedling that wilted and died had to be hers. I think her gloom must have had an effect for surely it could not all be laid at the door of others? One hardly dare ask after her plot knowing what you would probably learn. Offers of help, substitute plants, never seemed to be any good, she just seemed doomed to failure. Perhaps a little healthy optimism is necessary to successful growing. We all enjoy a little bit of "isn't it terrible?"-talk, some sympathy but not undiluted gloom and doom. Poor lady.

Thinking of substitute plants, the second try at keeping a borage plant has succeeded, the one left for me in the watering can. It has picked up with the help of its stick and is in full bright flower with new leaves appearing as well. Hopefully if I leave it alone it will seed itself below and provide me with new plants next year. What an intense and perfect blue the petals are.

Sunday

Decided that the angelica, now mostly brown and dead-looking should be tidied up so with the sharp kitchen knife, cut through the base of the plants across the huge stems. They were positively musical with their hollow "snap", as I sawed through, the wider the stem the deeper the note. The seedheads showered bits all over my hair. Carried the six foot stems up to the compost wondering if there was any positive use for the long hollow stems . . . a blowpipe maybe, or nose flute?

Have left some of the cut seedheads in a pile on the soil in the hope of a little controlled propogation.

★ ★ ★

Almost filled the cherry basket (Great Aunt Mary's) with purple french beans, it is a splendid crop. James noticed evidence of strange happenings with his beetroots, many chewed off tops lying strewn around. Wondered if someone had helped themselves but we think that it must be squirrels or some other four-footed delinquent.

★ ★ ★

Picked some rhubarb. The second crop is even better, about two foot long and tender with it. Will freeze some tomorrow as it is at its peak now. We do it free-flow in short pieces and then box or bag it. Some people sugar it a bit but we don't as it gets used for chutney as well as sweets.

Heard an owl, then the Parish striking 8 o'clock and made a damp exit.

Tuesday
The square patch of corn looks marvellous and really is "elephant's eye", or anyway is taller than James! Some of the lowest shoots do in fact have cobs forming and this backs up what Robbie said which was that you could pick them off earlier to help the plant concentrate its growing on flowers and cobs etc., but that in some seasons some might be productive. He is right!

The leeks left in their original seed row are nearly as thick as your little finger so a bit large for transplanting, anyway we have so many! The plotholder who roars up on a 1000 cc motor bike calls them "boy scout food", not sure what he means.

Thursday pm
Both had scissors and did a quick leek-snip of the planted out ones this evening. Picked some of the new spinach too, cutting across the whole plant as directed by James, rather than pulling a leaf here and there. This chumping seems to stimulate new growth to replace the cut stems.

* * *

Swifts zooming really low, head height almost. Seems an age since they have been sky-high specks catching insects in the warm air.

Grubbed some weeds down the tank end but hope to have a concerted attack (weather permitting) tomorrow before we go away. Ten days absence can give the weeds a "field-day" literally.

Saw tiniest frog in the tomato patch, so quick and brown, almost invisible.

Monday
After being away it all looks pretty shaggy
but have seen worse. Phil says that there
had not been a lot to harvest in fact
but had picked some french beans for
us, trimmed and frozen not blanched.
We took home a new picking of lovely
young runners, two basketfuls. Had a big
session sorting these and the french beans
and then blanched the lot, just for two
minutes . . . a good rinse to cool them
off, onto dry teacloths and bagged up.
All done in an hour, a satisfying task,
seeing all the nice, bright green shiny
bags waiting to be put into the freezer.
When we piled them in we found one bag
left over from last year . . . full circle!

Wednesday
More harvesting. Was able to walk
up inside the tunnel made by the
beanstick canopy. Always amazed to
find how many you miss and when James
follows on he has almost a full basketful
himself by the time he catches me up.
You walk up one way and pick, then
back the other making discoveries each
time. There seems to be more flowers

than leaves this year, the cool showery summer has suited most things, only the human consumers are less pleased with the shortage of real sunshine. Feel quite wan sometimes, maybe a vitamin D deficiency?

James dug up a bucket of potatoes, really clean in spite of the tacky soil. No one around and the whole site looks unkempt, 'depressed'! Orange posters are displayed announcing the annual show in early September. James pulled up a lettuce, very muddy. I said that I hoped it had no big slugs in it this time . . . "Oh no . . . " he says. Checked . . . enormous grey chap hanging on grimly with his frilly orange trimmings! "Give it to the thrush" he says when I complain. Bravely I throw it towards the bird, inaccurately but not far away. He or she ignores my gift and gets a brown wiry creature from the newly dug potato area. Maybe he'll indulge in my slug as a dessert after we have gone home. Not sure if they like slugs but hedgehogs do and the fox too.

★ ★ ★

The onions have reached full size and have been harvested, now drying in the greenhouse on the slats. 50 pounds from one pound of onion sets, not bad.

There is a blight on the gooseberry bushes and they will need drastic pruning this autumn but first to look up in the book what might be the present complaint, something has had a fine time gobbling up the leaves. The new blackcurrant bushes have now picked up after a rather slow start and have made ten inches in growth.

The exhibition secretary approached us, armed with yellow schedules, asking for some promise of contributions to the show, only 36 entries so far which is disappointing. We said "maybe" cautiously but I did promise to be a butterer behind the scenes to help the teas-people. Also we shall donate some sugar. Everyone is supposed to give a bit which helps the all over profits realised, these then go to the local hospice, a worthy cause.

Spent an hour and half doing beans for the freezer with some TV to help with the boredom threshold.

Saturday

Tied the topmost bit of the tomatoes which are fattening up nicely. Believe that it is the summer light, not necessarily the actual sunshine, that ripens them. Just as well as the weather is dreary, reverting yet again to more rain.

All the plots look shaggy and the edges badly need a trim.

Wednesday

Sadly, went to Peter's funeral this morning. It seems so sudden, unexpected. Only a few weeks ago we were talking together on the plot. He was on his way home and I was picking currants. He asked if we really liked them as his Kate did not but he did, and we made ourselves quite peckish speaking of cream and sugar, sorbets, delicious Summer puddings! He also talked to James and accepted from him a big bag of newly dug potatoes from the top plot. This was to be our last meeting.

We all go back a long way together, both of us having shared many student days, locally here and at college.

Now we stand apart from the chief

mourners who are grouped in the deep shade of a huge chestnut tree, already speckled with soft conkers. The green pretend grass thinly disguises the newly dug soil for the interrment. We have been to many cremations here, but never an actual burial. Alf joins us, unusually tidy and black-tied. We speak quietly of the service just over, the great number of people filling every seat, lining the chapel walls.

"Only seven at Mrs Willsher's" he compares.

If it was his burial, (Heaven help us!) we should all be the losers for as Hon. Sec. he brings a welcome humour to the site accompanied by enormous energy and enthusiasm. Although genial and appears to suffer fools gladly on the whole, nevertheless he has very high standards and keeps us all on our allotment toes. He uses the mechanical aids with zest and efficiency and has been the main reason for us taking on more plot. "You can do it" he says, so we do!

Kate joins us to speak bravely, say "thank you for coming" but I notice a tear stain dark on her grey silk blouse.

It is going to be hard for her.

Back home we are both thoughtful. Sometimes I wonder how I should cope on my own regarding plots. "Which one should I keep on?" I ask James who refuses to take me seriously of course. Then we argue over the various benefits and advantages . . . soft fruit bushes . . . better light . . . water tanks!

Sunday am
Sunny has had another stroke. Miss him on the allotment. Thought of them as we stopped for a drink from the Thermos and a bit of fruit cake. The couple often used to spend the whole day there, their wooden seat set against the brick wall ready for well-earned rest times. Beattie usually had a fag in her mouth and her cough was awful but she was always cheerful even when Sunny became glum and unwell, only able to watch her working away on their plot, envious and frustrated.

Sat on my new kneeler-seat which is proving useful except when muddy, then I sink in and it is more trouble than help!

Mystery . . . the packet of "Everlasting" seem to have produced three different kinds of plants, which is the right kind? Have given Phil some from the same packet so must warn her of possible "cuckoos".

Tuesday
Mystery solved as I have now checked the packet which actually contains three different kinds of everlasting! Saw on TV how to pick and dry them with cones of newspaper hung up in a cool dry place. May need wiring to avoid floppy heads they said.

Thursday
Last night's heavy showers have beaten down the everlasting plants sadly, not sure if they will recover. Very low light today, heavy clouds, headachey weather but no rain since the downpour last night. The hoe is no use at all, too sticky. All very still . . . no rustling, no birdsong.

Flying ants on the path. Tickled for hours afterwards slapping imaginary crawlers inside our clothes.

Saturday
Slaughtered the herbs, using the shears as well as my secateurs, having a real trim-day. Bees a bit of a problem as there are still a few flowers left on some of the clumps. A nice, aromatic job . . . artemesia, lavender, rosemary, thyme, marjoram, hyssop, lovely clean sweet smells.

Late afternoon visit to the plot, still very hot, but less sultry, a bit of a breeze. Not many there, but saw Winnie in the distance. She has achieved a harvest of 75 pounds of runner beans nearing her record of 98!

James dug up the four tatty lupins by the herb garden, amazingly long roots. The drought and greenfly have wrought havoc with them this year and we have decided to take them all out. The new rosemary bush, a cutting, seems very slow to get bigger but looks sturdy. Have planted it beside the second lavender so that with the plentiful artemisia cuttings it can, eventually and hopefully, form a hedge-strip, a little like an Elizabethan garden. I have moved the lavender twice already, changing my mind about its position but it seems content now and has put out two spikes of flowers, deep blue. The feverfew is sowing itself all over the place which is good . . . We like its brightness and the bees like the flowers. The air is full of scents, bruised thyme, verbena, mint, and the celery smell of lovage. The new leaves already show above the earth and I use the shears to take off the older stuff, by the time the cooler early autumn days come the regrowth is sturdy. I took the cut rubbish up to the shared compost pile near the park fence, a positive mountain now. The hives seemed quiet, it is live and let live arrangement and some still buzzed around the cut herbs as I left. Anyway, there are masses of red and cream runner bean flowers for them. Percy has cream ones, says they should not need any stringing.

★ ★ ★

Mrs Somme asked me to identify a herb she had been given, although I am no expert. She chewed a bit of the grey-green leaf but soon spat it out. We both thought it might be rue. "Do you use your herbs much?" she asked. I confessed that I grew them as much for their look and scent as for their culinary use but did include the odd leaf in a casserole or salad, and certainly the fennel with fish. James does not like the aniseedy taste but I do and Mrs Somme said that she was going to make a fennel sauce that very day. She is a great lady we think and admire her perseverance with her plot. However we do not care for her slug slaughter system which results in jam jars full of wet rotting and very malodorous corpses! She had come on her bike today but drives a car as well. Very dismissive about a recent ramble she had been on, "they took half an hour to walk one mile so I left them to it".

Wednesday
Winnie stopped for a chat and we talked about the lack of birdsong now. She had seen the sparrow hawk's chicks fly off she said. I wish we had. The parents have squeaked and hovered over the allotments all summer it seemed . . . all gone now. Winnie says that she has been

talking to an 'orphan' robin. Not sure how she knows that it is one. Miss the swifts, all departed now.

★ ★ ★

The young bee-couple have got another baby! A gorgeous little boy of four months. "Has held us back a bit," they said but were obviously adoring. Carried the little one in his pouch up the path to visit their hives with the older, but not much older son, to introduce the new arrival we supposed. Possibly a birth should be duly notified as well as a death?

When they returned they brewed up in the van and had a snack before the father went back to the hives leaving his family to suck or play, peacefully.

September

Sunday

A BIT of proper rain at last. Only harvested today, plenty of the purple climbing runners, so much easier to gather than the back-breaking low bush kind. If we pick them as soon as they are just full size they need no stringing too, just cutting up into pieces. They go into the boiling water dark purple and then change to green in minutes, leaving the stock green too so where does the purple go? The runner beans are tough and hard with the lack of rain lately so they need a lot of drastic stringing and fine slicing.

The tomatoes are lush, (had plenty of regular watering) but still green, both leaves and fruits with just the occasional near-ripening one showing a little orange tinge.

Mr Glum (by nature) gloomily commented on their colour and James tried to convince him, probably unsuccessfully, that all would ripen eventually, if not on plant, certainly in a drawer. "Put a ripe tomato in with the green ones and this gives them the right idea". We do not know why exactly but it appears to work. Maybe some chemical is given off by the red one?

pm
Felt chilly for the first time in many months. There was a splendid pink and gold sunset. The light seem to fade as we left for home, the last to go in a true dusk. No birdsong, no fox, (no bats for Miss Tear's boxes).

Sadly a lady in one of the nearby houses had died recently. She used to feed the vixen regularly and it still calls at the gate, their own entrance straight into the allotments. The widower rattles the catch and she comes to feed, not minding the change of hand, a man's smell and voice, too hungry to be particular.

Made my "allotment" jam, a kind of cheese I am told, not a true jelly. I don't strain it through my old Harrington nappy, now a brownish-pink with years of quince, blackberry, currant juices trickling through it, suspended on an upturned stool, dripping all night. The sludge goes into the compost bin so nothing wasted . . . the great recycle! I have got a juice extractor fitting on my new food processor but when we first used it James spent so long cleaning out the pippy bits we both wondered if the old fashioned method was not simpler, if slower.

Despair of my marrow and ginger jam ever setting, I have boiled it up twice now and am afraid it will be a case of "sauce" for a pudding, only as James cannot abide ginger it will be up to me to get rid of it, I can hardly offer it to friends in this state.

Heard a tale of the site today, from Lily, of "Rocky" who was the local coalman who had her plot before she did. He used to give the Truelove lads (before they grew up to be plumbers), rides in his horse-driven coal-cart, a genial, cheerful man of character. A little man but obviously strong, he always wore a bright neckerchief and called himself the "last poor man in B . . . ham". He had his own particular way of getting rid of the weeds on his plot. He would trundle his homemade cart on pram wheels to the local builder's yard near his home in Limes Road and get a stack of small offcuts. These he brought back to the allotments piling them on top of his weedy patches. Then he set them alight. Lily, who lived as now, adjacent to the site used to have to time her washdays with care as the sooty smoke could be a disaster! She took over his plot when it had become too much for him, now in his eighties, (even with a scorched earth system), and reckoned she had a very good potash content but, on the debit side, an even better crop of nettles, which grow, they say, where the ground is "good"!

Rocky was devoted to his "Mum", and Lily used to watch him as he prepared for one of his visits to her. He would wander up and down the allotments, sizing up the flower-stocks. Then, with no apparent conscience, he would gather a great bunch of flowers . . . only the best "for Mum"!

The muddy welly-boot is a great

leveller. Plotholders help each other with various expertise, like the Truelove brothers, sons of the local blacksmith, (now grown-up, plumbers both), making Lily a permanent bean frame from spare piping. A carpenter knocked up 'boxes' to individual plotholder's specifications bearing in mind that we may not have . . . "Any erections above two feet" as stipulated in the site rule book. We were curious to know why one plotholder was referred to as the "bloody fireman" . . . what offence had he given? But it turned out that a fellow plotholder was a surgeon and that he had had to do an emergency operating job on the fireman in a London hospital one day. He had never known such a copious "bleeder" he said.

Tuesday
Resolution, to catch up on tidying jobs. Rain was good but it needs a real prolonged soak as the upper plot is still quite dry underneath the top soil. Untidy plots, bolting lettuces, runner beans tailing off now and yellowing, mildewy

mint. The water tank is surfaced with whizzing water boatmen playing noughts and crosses on the green reflections. The robin is soon with us. It is a lovely day, warm sunshine, clear skies. We have harvested some small beetroots, sweet and less costly to cook. Freezing them last year was not a success as they went all collapsed and soggy as they thawed out.

Staked up the brussel sprout plants as they are getting a bit of a list already but most are healthy and upright.

Saturday
Another good day. Trimmed the leek plants, counted 52 in one row only! That is an awful lot of leeks. None get wasted though with generous helpings and (windy) soup concoctions.

I noticed that the new sage bush was getting swamped by buttercups and nettles so put on gloves to clear some away and free it. The gap between gloves and dress sleeve meant a lot of stinging and the tingle will stay all day I expect, but it is so warm who wants to be covered up!

James dug up a sack of potatoes. We shall be glad of these as they say that prices will be high this year due to the wet cold Spring. Must get a new seed list from the hut on Sunday.

Had a great harvest-time. The gourds are almost finished and there are trays of them all over the house, drying out. We bought two custard marrows (white and scalloped) from the famous Slindon lady near Chichester and hope to save their seeds if possible. Bought a booklet too from her stall, all about squashes and gourds with recipes, these will prove useful if our two, great golden pumpkins progress and we manage to keep the slugs away.

The beans keep on making their positively "last appearance"! Some quite small and tender, post rain crop. Some James will leave to ripen for seed. There have been golden days and grey days this month but it is a good time, new buds are pushing off the old leaves and you get a sense of ongoing things, almost more than at Eastertide.

Saturday

Such a beautiful day, warm, light breeze, clear sky, quite perfect. Surprisingly few people about. Crickets or grasshoppers were chirruping in the near 'meadow' beside our plot. The newcomer is doing well, working sensibly and thoroughly, slowly, in stages. The top of his plot is still wild and has a lot of scarlet pimpernel, (such a pretty "wildflower" but you can only really appreciate it when down close). Today we harvested more potatoes, a whole row of whites, hard work! Were puzzled by the occasional single red Desiree amongst them, maybe a leftover from two years ago as last year we had rotated as usual and had brassicas there. Counted thirteen potatoes from one plant. The littlest button sized ones got thrown, I am ashamed to say, far into the missing young man's plot! Seems ungracious but if you could see the sorry state of his allotment you would understand . . . a few selfsown potatoes will make little or no difference. The weeds are several feet high and seeding all over any plot breeze-distance away. He must have gone abroad again.

The soil was so crumbly in the potato trenches that we were able to weed as we went, so the area already looks ready for the next move . . . "muck" says James.

Tuesday
The new raspberry canes put in last weekend look all right except for three which seem a little traumatised still. They make nearly another full row and the established ones, thinned out and tied, are neat and orderly. In fact the whole plot has suddenly become quite disciplined and the huge weed growth slowed down now it is mid September.

Two rows of parsley are through! Winnie said sow when the soil is warm so they went in in mid August, and there they are. Well pleased.

Sat in the garden after late lunch and prepared vegetables for the freezer . . . purple french beans, late runners, and some early little walnuts of brussels. There is a great basket of apple windfalls waiting to be attended to but they will have to wait their turn. They scent the kitchen to remind me to hurry up before they go all wrinkly and past their best.

The garden apple tree was supposed to be a half standard Cox but turned out to be a Worcester and they do not keep well.

Wasps came to inspect our lunch plates left on the grass. We have had a nest under the eaves by the porch. The exterminator man told us that once the queen was isolated all that was needed was some of his deadly spray-stuff. But when we came back from the plot the next day, we saw the big queen near the hole and had to kill her. The same week we discovered a great funnel-hole in our compost heap on the plot. There was much comings and goings with the busy wasp colony and we decided to leave them be and pile up any new rubbish at the side rather than over their entrance. The exterminator said that at this time of year wasps are dying off naturally and we will soon be able to turn the heap over or burn it and I suppose cremate the queen. We found an old nest in our loft soon after we moved into this house, a wonderful intricate affair. Mrs Somme said that the one she had on her compost heap was made from chewed up pink Financial Times, very selective! Ours appear to be less classy and all we can see is an earthy funnel-end among the weeds and rhubarb leaves.

Thursday
The water tanks look murky and when we noticed a dog having a drink apparently enjoying it, we thought it must be a kind of canine "cocktail". I forgot the watering can the other night so filled my Safeways carrier, (surprised how much it takes), made some small holes with a twig and did a dainty douche on the things that needed a water most. Must remember not to use that particular bag for harvesting.

Several tomatoes are ready to pick and a good size. Skinned some that had been ripening on the kitchen window sill, warm from the sun and the flavour was delicious. Fresh basil is a treat but my potted plant is nearly used up now sadly. Wish we could have it as a perennial but it is too cold even here in the South-East and I am told that the hardier type is more bitter and less aromatic anyway. Have discovered a bottled green paste, basil-based which is not cheap but makes a real aristocrat of homemade tomato soup.

Monday
Pig manure from Keston this year. 12 yards dumped in the car park at the weekend. Had to be divided up into fair one yard piles so we made a start this evening. Many trips with the wheelbarrow with steaming ammoniac piles, James soon steaming too and the interested wasps making the job even less pleasant. The trouble was that you had to negotiate a couple of right-hand turns with an uneven pathway so with non aligned plots and hollow tracks it was not an easy exercise. We decided that it was 100 yards there, another 100 back and about 10 sorties each! Good stuff though, only a few straw bits and the odd brick or stone. A

robin came to enjoy the juicy things around the edge of the pile, (what James and the stables lady call "the gravy"). Discovered a blister on my palm and felt quite proud to have been useful having been told initially, to "Just come and watch" for company. Had decided to bring the small border fork and keep up as best I could, in fact enjoyed positive action rather than spectating. Too weary to even pick sprouts and expect a few aches and pains tomorrow.

Saturday
The children here for the day. Went up twice, once to pick sprouts for our lunch, then later to do a little combined work. The last bonus bean flowers have not had to suffer any frosts yet, even though it will be October next week, and there were a few still to pick. The recent days have been warm and dry and although the leaf-fall is getting greater, (particularly the chestnuts in the park), the air is benign, kindly, except for one sullen Tuesday last week when it became all grey and still, the leaves limp and

completely motionless . . . much prefer the livelier days.

Tuesday
Could not use the compost heap properly as the wasps were still too busy around it. In the house there are bodies appearing everywhere. Up the plot they seem to be committing kamikaze in the water tanks alongside other winged creatures.

Quite a nice day but heavy, it seems to swing from sunny to sullen these early autumn weeks but the leaves are spinning down from the park beech and sycamore trees.

An old lady of 86 told me that it was lucky to catch the first falling leaf of autumn. I don't know how you know it is the first . . . the first you see yourself floating down perhaps! Anyway, I caught mine and made my wish!

Saturday
September is always marked by the annual District Allotments show or late August sometimes, and we always hope not to miss it, be away that particular weekend.

Last year it was held in the hall of my old school. It was much changed of course and I had not been back there for many many years. In fact the last time had been a "reunion" when I vowed never to attend such a gathering again, not my cup of tea at all, . . . all that looking back and swapping how many children; aborted or successful "careers"; . . . deaths and disappointments, countered with smug self satisfaction. Was I the only one to wish myself elsewhere after the first five minutes?

★ ★ ★

When we arrived this day last year, we approached the hall by the gravel path that took you past what had been in my time, the Head Mistress' study. When as schoolchildren we had our playtime on the grass outside we would be very careful to keep our silliness out of sight of her forbidding, observing, gaze. I noticed that the still huge tulip tree was there, dominating the lawn, and at the darker far end of the area, the cluster of pine trees, rising out of their dusty, needled ground, backed by shrubs ideal for concealment and exclusive, childish "clubs". These clannish often cruel, games meant misery for some, as already the seeds of leadership and discrimination had been laid . . . "Them" and "Us" I remembered all too well.

The two grass tennis courts had gone, replaced now by a red brick block of retirement flats, and the rose walk and gardens, (a leftover in my schooldays of the real garden belonging to the Georgian house), had also gone, making way for practical single-storey classrooms.

But the actual corridor we follow, down to the hall, is almost exactly the same . . . ("Don't run girls, WALK!"), and only lacks the shiny black metal coat hooks, thoughtfully graded in height for each growing year, and the rows of wooden shoe-lockers. I remembered my own brown cloth shoe-bag with its initials embroidered by my mother in green silk laisy-daisy, "N. L. J."

The school hall smells of fruit and veg., heady and sweet. The rain unseasonally teems down the big panes of glass, blurring our view of the grounds outside. On the platform sits our Chairman, in his nineties but going strong even if now wheelchair-bound.

The selfsame platform had been where all our plays and concerts took place, times of huge excitement out of all proportion to the event! Anguish; forgotten lines; the sea of faces looking up at you with great expectations; pride; envy. The Prize-givings! I still have books with pasted-in commendations to remind me of that long walk up to the steps, and up the steps (and down again) to collect the award . . . "Music"; "Art"; "English"; you could see even then that I was going on a slippery path of no return! And yet the prize I value most I think is a metal spoon that has long since lost its "silver", now true honest brass. I had joined a ladies swimming club very much a beginner, and after about a year our Hon. Sec. called me over to the side of the pool to tell me that I should be receiving the annual award "for best progress" . . . being dismally lacking in confidence of most things physical, this was for me, an unexpected and great personal triumph!

My earliest use of the school hall though was the dancing class, an "extra". One girl, (envied by us) had an individual lesson probably a lot more costly, and we would have to queue up outside the hall door waiting for her spoiled spiralling to stop before we were allowed to troop in.

Mothers were permitted to watch their little darlings but sat in quiet submission knowing that Miss Ayling would give them a taste of her disapproval if a single word was uttered during her class.

We responded each in our own way to the teachings of Miss Ayling in varying degrees of ineptitude or grace, adoring and fearing her. Finally, we would line up to approach her in two reverent columns, to execute our statutory wobbly curtsey, saying "Thank you Miss Ayling" before leaving the hall, keeping in step to the lady pianist's march, the tempo suitably timed for our small paces.

Now the scent of Miss Ayling's cologne and the fresh polish on the linoleumed floor is replaced by earthier wafts of onions, cabbages and chrysanths.

This year, in another place, people have been toiling last night and in the early hours of this Saturday morning to prepare everything for the annual show. The local purpose-built boy's school is better equipped for the event and I have done my bit as "chief butterer" in the spacious school kitchen! Exhibits inclined to wilt are brought in at the last minute but the judging takes place midday and all has to be ready before 10.30am. The many trestle tables are arranged in the hall for all the categories . . . vegetable classes of every kind, individuals and Inter-Group;

"Novices" . . . (we could enter this in fact, even with all those years tucked under our belts, as we qualify being " . . . a member who has not taken a First prize for vegetables at any Allotment or Horticultural Show"). Then there are the flowers, Open classes with miniature and thematic arrangements; Dahlia classes; Chrysanthemum classes. And what about the "Novelty" classes . . . Heaviest Onion; Biggest Marrow; Longest Runner Bean; all quite inedible of course!

The Domestic class involves cakes and preserves, wines too and I have entered for this, winning a First for my chutney one year, but as there were only 3 entries in all didn't feel too big headed and collected £1 with suitable modesty. (The collecting box for the local Hospice placed on the table where the cups sit and the awards are given out, does well. Most of the "prizes" are token and winners are glad to pass them on in a good cause).

At midday the judging begins but of course we are not allowed to witness it. We have had our schedules, entered our exhibits, (read the rules!) and now it is in the lap of the Show Gods . . .

The annual battle of the sites is about to begin! On the whole, it is friendly rivalry but some do take the whole affair seriously, perhaps too much so.

When we are allowed in for the official opening at 3pm we soon get going on our rounds to see who has been successful and won a prize or commendation.

I take time off from my sandwich-making and join James in disagreeing with the "experts" and questioning (not too loudly) the handwritten comments on the tickest displayed by the entries. In the Domestic classes we read. "Too pippy . . . "; "Too sweet . . . "; "A little slack . . . ".

Displayed on pretty doyleys are mouth-watering meringues stuffed with cream; sponges with cobwebbed icing; Victorias bleeding raspberry jam; all with their sample slice missing, (lucky judges), spoiling their prettiness. Likewise the golden quiches and collapsed Pavlovas.

The pots of jam and pickles have also had their trial scoop taken and the results lie in coloured tickets beside the jars. It is good that we all do in fact have a go, as all the points gained are added up, going towards a site total, and we (our site) want to repeat our success of last year with "Best in the Borough"!

Each site can enter a combined tray of eight mixed vegetables and although we total eleven sites only a few take part. Our own pumpkin graced the tray last year but we have nothing this time. Once Robbie, looking for the best produce on the site, pulled up several of our carrots in search of perfection and we returned from a holiday to find them, discarded, rejected drying out on the earth!

We walk up and down the rows of trestles, admiring, criticising, disagreeing, ("our beetroots are better than those surely?"). The blackberry exhibits always look so pretty especially the thornless variety ("not less than 24, with stalks") . . . arranged on their frilly dark green leaves. Percy was away this weekend but Alf had entered for him, a selection of his late raspberries and they had won him a "first", well deserved we thought, agreeing with the judges this time. A few days ago when we were changing our shoes in the car park, we noticed someone up by Percy's plot and saw him pick and eat more than half a dozen of the fruits! Still, there must have been enough for the entry and we shall not give him away unless Percy thinks that we have been the culprits when he returns!

★ ★ ★

There are other elegant arrangements such as the shallot entries, all identical sizes, the roots removed, the tops trimmed and neatly tied down with raffia. They sit on their bed of sawdust, golden-brown globes, all prize-winners as far as we are concerned. In fact we both prefer these vegetable displays to the formal flower arrangements. These scent the hall and demand attention with their brilliant colours but somehow you long for more subtlety, less strong contrasts, less "Borough planting colours" as James calls them. He dislikes as I do, the juxtaposition of lobelia, salvia and French marigolds on the traffic islands.

The dahlias with their stiffly spiked petals or honeycombed centres remind me of a sweet shop we saw in Bruges, all those sugary patterned "pom-poms". But the roses are always lovely and there are challenging themes for mixed flower arrangements such as "Setting Sun" . . . "The News"? . . . I always intend to try for the miniature class, "Six inches maximum in any direction" but as yet have not got around to it. Better stick to useful buttering.

When we have a break I join James, who has been manning the produce stall, and we sample my sandwiches and homemade cakes with our cups of tea. With plotholder friends we discuss rather gloomily the latest rumour regarding the loss of our site, this in spite of the local M. P.'s assurances at the official opening, that everyone appreciated the many values of allotmenteering. "My father had one . . . " (It is funny how everybody official seems to have a father, or grandfather who shares our love of plotholding, but of, course, "they" never have the time!)

We are joined at our table by a parent and her two boys. It turns out that they are the two, (almost only), "Children's

Class" entrants. There are in fact seven categories including, "A Buttonhole for Mother"; "Six Rock Cakes"; "A Piece of Handicraft"; and a usually amusing, "Animal or Bird made from fruit and/or vegetables". Between them these two lads had almost swept the board with their, no doubt egged-on, endeavours as only two other names appeared on the displays. However, the respective judges had shown great tact and understanding of the nature of sibling rivalry, equally distributing the first and seconds with care. We hope that more children will be encouraged to take part, maybe the names of young Amy and her like will appear in future years.

* * *

The annual battle is over . . . the exhibits sold off, the happy and disgruntled depart. At home eating up some of the ham left over from the teas, James and I mull over the programme and he reads aloud . . . "Fancy an allotment? Fresh veg. and green fingers? Healthy Exercise and Friendship? Occasional Lectures &

Outings?" ("Don't remember any of those") . . . "Eleven sites and over 600 plots for rent at a very reasonable cost". This is certainly true even with seeds to buy, and muck.

"Did you ever see sweet corn growing on Mick's plot?" asks James, "He got a first though!"

"First Class refreshments" ("Thank you"), "and the renewal of old friendships and true Show spirit" . . . we agree. Our lucky number programme has not proved lucky for us but certainly we have enjoyed very much, this special occasion.

October

SPREAD some of the muck. Sunny and Beattie were up the top, he still poorly, sitting, bowed over on their wooden seat, looking really disconsolate while Beattie dug up their last row of potatoes. She had a bucket of water beside her and popped the earthy potatoes straight in. A good idea as then you could swish off some of the dirt before taking them home. James went up for a chat and to give her a hand.

It was warm working. The plot looks unkempt but it is not just us but a general site-look.

Concorde went over our heads, more • heard than seen today with the low cloud.

Sunday
Masses of really solid brussels sprouts. The plants are shorter, sturdier this year

and are doing really well. The leeks that did not get their trim look no different from the shorter, chopped ones which makes you wonder how necessary it is to do this chore.

The beech nuts are hitting the corrugated iron roof of the allotment shed, a staccato timpani, almost a positive tune with an accompaniment of a squirrel's jittery call.

Saw a big golden toad, big enough to avoid as we are always fearful of hurting the smaller, hidden ones.

The tomatoes are all finished except a few small ones. Must do a whole host of jobs, prune the gooseberry bushes to "let the air in . . . ", sow the broad beans for an early crop and plant the garlic.

Sometimes differ over the value of growing carrots but have to admit that this year it has been much better. If not quite as smooth as the supermarket ones, these are pretty fair and a lovely strong flavour. James tells me to firm down the earth well where I have pulled the carrots, so that the wigglies and chewers do not have a field-day in the gaps.

Wednesday
The Jerusalem artichokes are collapsing but are still quite green. Wretched things to clean for cooking but as we have so many, take the lazy way and after washing and scrubbing the knotty tubers, boil them until tender, cool and then skin them. You do lose a bit of the flesh but we can afford to be wasteful. No doubt the poor Victorian scullery maid would have the onerous job of actually peeling them first!

★ ★ ★

Reviewing our top grassy area, we feel that it has proved its worth as we have actually spent quite a lot of time up there this year, albeit briefly, taking a welcome breather.

Have definitely decided to move the daisies to a higher sunnier spot but will leave the iris where they are. We have added donations of some montbretia to our crinum and the Peruvian lilies so it may become a rather interesting corner. What with this, the growing herb garden, the roses and our "lawn" I can see that we are beginning to show signs of old age! The older you grow, the less you grow, and the number of fruit bushes, flowers and raspberry canes increase! Still, why shouldn't the plot be both pretty and productive. Look nice, smell nice, as well as taste good? Anyway, the bees love it.

Tuesday pm
Cleared the tomato area while James did some digging. Quite an exercise with removing the protective sheets of rigid plastic and their canes first, then the plant supports. Separating the canes from the tight strings is never easy, but this year we have used plastic ties of one kind or another, and this has made the

job much less frustrating. It reminds me of trying to remove a too-tight wedding ring! I end up with a pocketful of ties and chewed-up thumbnail after over fifty "twists" but still better than having to saw through endless damp-tightened strings.

Last year we had a deluge just before the tomatoes were finished and the weight of the trusses and the water made several of the plants actually snap. We came back from a few days break to find them leaning one on another and the trusses overflowing the plastic sheets. Mr Glum says "Only fit for chutney" but we ignored this Jeremiah attitude as most of the fruits will ripen quite well indoors.

Found a hidden marrow near the water tank, the shaggy grass verge had kept it out of sight and it had grown so huge that I needed both hands to lift it up! The skin was soft though not tough at all.

Saturday
Some ripening blackberries around, some crimson and still useable. All the garden apples are finished now so I have no

need of adding the berries to pink them up. What we don't eat I'll freeze and make into sorbets, or winter, "Summer" puddings for special occasions. The plot-mixture jam has been well received and when I have a collection of small honey jars filled with this nice, solid 'cheese' can arrive as guest, not empty-handed. It is so reliable resetting, unlike that wretched marrow and ginger concoction which is still lurking, unused in my preserves cupboard.

Sunday
A strong wind tonight made us look back to another October and that awful gale. We had lain awake all night, flinching as the great buffeting gusts hit the bedroom window until we could stand it no longer, retreating to the spare room in the front of the house. We pulled the covers over our heads and didn't sleep at all even though it was a little quieter there, but the noise of the snapping and groaning of the trees was really frightening. The next day we went up to the allotments and were met with a terrible sight. The biggest beech tree in the park, among

others had fallen down, right across our plots diagonally, it could not have been worse. Only the very top part was unscathed and poor Mrs Sommes's plot had disappeared almost entirely.

The huge silvery trunk seen close to, was ten times bigger than when it stood upright, and the shorter branches were driven deep into the soil. All the soft fruits were smashed, gone, and the whole area of the carefully planted out leeks disappeared. There were beech nuts everywhere scrunching underfoot and twigs, whole snapped off branches, a disaster area. Trying to look for a blessing in disguise, near to tears we decided that at least, once cleared, we would be able to make a fresh start in that lower area, but comments from other less unfortunate plotholders did not go down well, we could have done with less commiseration and more positive help.

"What a disaster!" . . . "You've got a lot on your plate!" . . . "What an enormous tree . . . !" It was the end of March before the park people came and sawed off the big trunk where it lay, a great carcase. It had crushed the link fence, intruding on our plots although by then we had managed slowly to reclaim some of the earth. We found, amazingly, soft fruit bushes surviving where the angle of the smaller fallen branches had protected them a little, others not so lucky. The sawn trunk now revealed a great rotten centre, a cavern and Mrs Somme had the great idea of using this as an incinerator. Week after week we all had this localised bonfire and gradually it ate away the surrounding wood. The park people had left great piles of logs too and these were stuffed in so that you would go up the next day and find the fire still smouldering, ready for the next attack. The shed had been crushed too and every visit after the gale we would pick up twigs, branches, the debris of the wind. It was a depressing time but you just had to get on with things.

The second lot of gales, in January this time, did its worst and to our dismay, brought down two more trees on our plots. These were as tall if not as thick as the old beech, this time, an oak and a sycamore. So we start all over again and as the rainfall had been great at that time, had to cope with a sea of mud as well as great branches and trunks. The family came to help one weekend and we had two huge great bonfires in the car park. The townhouse people no doubt grumbled but we were in no mood for the complaints of others. It was clean wood smoke anyway, pungent but not unpleasant except to our eyes if we misjudged the prevailing wind. Gradually the great dents were filled, the crops replaced, the new stakes put in place and it became just a tale told.

When the park team came eventually a mini-drama happened as one man was using a power saw. He suddenly threw it down, running away from the trunk at full speed yelling and batting about. Evidently he had cut right through a bees nest and they had woken up exceedingly angry!

Saturday
Not much birdsong just a warning chink from a blackbird and a bit of a trill from an out-of-sight robin. Three seagulls circled above us in a sky pretty with mackerel clouds. As well as seagulls,

planes were buzzing around all afternoon, jolly two-engined ones, jets flying much higher, crisscrossing the allotment site.

November

Monday

THE seed orders have arrived and await our collection. Robbie complains that people don't come and pick them up until they have been nagged. "Don't they want them" he sighs.

James is in his bad books as he filled in his form wrongly it seems and there was some mix-up but I expect Alf ironed it out and smoothed ruffled feathers as usual.

A lot of Robbie's noble work must be very tedious and he has the added burdens of managing the total eleven sites, all that paper work.

Who will be there to fight our battles with the Council? We may need someone like him in the future to protect our own site from greedy speculators, slavering over our delectable site, a perfect acreage for a mini-estate of Tudorbethan dwellings. (And money in some unscrupulous official's pocket. Even the Head of Social Services has disappeared under a cloud to a convenient tax haven!)

Alf on his gloomier days, reckons that our loss is inevitable if not imminent, and says that we should all make sure that our loss would be seen as "a bloody crying shame". It is such a pocket of peace, an oasis in a suburban desert, even a sanity-saver! Cups and awards are not the criteria of good allotmenteering for most of us, but we see his point, a few shining accolades, a County placing, might serve their purpose in giving us a credibility and superficial clout in a threatened future.

Saturday
A wedding was being celebrated at the Parish with jolly bells but otherwise all was quiet, enough to actually hear the sound of leaves falling.

There are still a few scars left as reminders of the bad winds, gaps in rows of raspberries and currants; a tabby cat sitting on the fallen trunk of the beech tree. Once swamping us, it is now diminished, chopped, sawn, burned away and the last rooted end-piece lies the other side of the new link fence, an obstruction to be climbed over by people walking in the park and their dogs using the upper path in the wilder wooded area alongside us.

★ ★ ★

Found two hidden and attractive gourds and a golf ball, very odd the latter as apart from the summertime clock golf in the children's park area, our nearest public course is all of two miles away!

Parsnips are improving, dug up quite a few. Mrs Somme has taken on yet another piece of plot! She is making a really good job of it despite the fact that she says "THEY" don't approve of her methods. It may look patchy with black plastic bits, old carpet, jars and boxes, but it is very productive and cared-for and many other more conventional plotholders could learn from her!

It is still quite mild but getting damp and the chill is nearing. Picked some

brussels that were full of rainwater. ("Start at the bottom" I am told . . . "I know" I reply as usual, as I give the plants a good shake before picking as I don't want the water running up my sleeve). Whilst James dug I cleared the runner beans, leaving the roots in as we do, (for nitrogen) but pulling up the poles and sliding the old material up to the narrow end and then off. A quick snip with the scissors and one done. It takes a while but I end up with the dried old stuff piled and ready to be burned or composted, neat stacks of sticks and some string for binding them. Made two bundles all earthy ends together and slanted them to rest up against the permanent metal poles, (the children's old climbing frame, rusty but useful). I wait for the taller James to come later and lift them up, laying them horizontally along the top rail. This keeps them neatly stacked until we need them next season and away from others temptations. We think it looks like a Red Indian burial structure, set on sacred ground, which, in a way, it is, to us anyway.

Remembrance Sunday

Had some of the blackberry cheese on crumpets for tea. Cheered up a drizzly grey day, always sad with moments of silence that few now respect. Grandma would never sing the line of the hymn which says "They fly forgotten as a dream dies at the opening day . . . " She would never forget her elder son, only 18 and lost over France, flying his Camel plane alone. She could never come to terms with the hymn's words or the Immaculate Conception and this worried her. A more delightful lovely person you could hardly find and I am quite certain that it did not matter in the least. If there is a Heaven then it would be a poorer place without her.

Wednesday

Have been surrounded by boxes and bowls full of ripening tomatoes but nearly at an end now. Delighted with Lily's tip for storing them. We have done as she said, skinned, pulped then frozen them in the ice cube trays. It takes a while but is well worth the effort. "Fresh" tomato soup on a winter's day is a treat and the cubes can be taken as many as you need, rather than have a great lump of iced tomato to thaw. The house reeks of vinegar but there is the pleasant sight of two rows of jars full of brown sweet chutney, to make it all worthwhile. Should ideally be left to 'mature' but soon goes.

Mrs Somme thought that she had mislaid her handbag the other evening. We all hunted high and low for it but without success.

She is a little prone these days to losing things and we are often asked to lookout for secateurs, fork, even anoraks and keys! Sensibly she usually wears the latter hung on a cord around her neck. The handbag was discovered later by Winnie right at the top of the site, all chewed up. Several days later the plastic-covered driving licence turned up, right by the townhouse end. Winnie says she once saw a fox leaping up and down in an attempt to reach her leather handbag hanging from a fruit-cage pole. What is it that attracts them? Is there nutritional value in chewed-up leather?

December

MUCK delivery. Should have come yesterday but Mr Potts "Couldn't get at it". Better day today with only a light drizzle but this got heavier as the load was being shifted from van to plot via the car park. Bagged muck is so much easier to handle but James reckoned that this particular load was a better buy.

The ground is saturated and digging really hard work. One measly frost is all we have had so far and we need more to help break up the earth. Nearly all the leaves seem to be down now and the hellebores are beginning to break into bloom. This is their great merit as you appreciate so much their brightness when everything else seems to be giving up or at least, resting. It is a pity that the purple flowers hang down their pretty heads when fully out, so that you have to gently lift each one to enjoy the full beauty of their inner markings, their delicate, decorative centres.

The euphorbia too is bright with its glossy green foliage but I regard the plant warily having had a very nasty experience one summer, coming out in a dreadful, body-covering rash just before we went on holiday. The awful irritation was so bad that I ended up at the surgery pleading for help and was immediately put onto a course of steroids. We never knew if the plant was the cause but could think of nothing else to blame at that time and I had been in contact with it, cutting off the flowerheads that week if not that actual day.

* * *

The holly berries are disappearing fast even though it is quite mild still, so some birds must be enjoying them.

The robin's song is miniscule, a tiny threadlike trill which cannot be focussed so that you are quite startled to find it right beside you, perched on the wheelbarrow, down by your foot. One evening though, at dusk, I was surprised to identify a robin by our back gate high up in the sycamore tree, trilling away in a much louder, maybe territorial song? Entirely different in shape and volume from his plot counterpart.

★ ★ ★

What makes twenty or more sparrows all gather together in a neighbour's vast bay tree, squabbling and fluttering loudly? A kind of sparrow's committee meeting? Union meeting, everyone shouting and no one listening!

Saw the woodpecker again on the nutfeeder, red crest, red underbelly, stabbing fiercely with his efficent beak. The mesh survives him and also beats one of our parakeets. There is one with a stronger than usual beak, who can do a proper snip job when he chooses, and this is why James has had to replace Mark One with Mark Two.

Monday
Percy's visit to the plots coincided with ours again but he didn't stay long this

time. It was too damp for him to sit and rest on his chair and one cigarette's length was his limit today. He is a little frail since his heart attack and completed his leek pulling in his own leisurely time.

"For soup I believe" he told James, obviously sent to get them for his wife's menu-plan. They discussed the moving of the late fruiting raspberry plants as he has promised us some more. No staking, (no prickles like the blackberry), just picking and eating hopefully.

★ ★ ★

The herbs need a huge thinning out, maybe some replanting but the muddy conditions deter me. Instead I trim the artemesia bushes and the rosemary but am a little concerned that the latter is dead-looking, at least half of it. I don't know why. I have hard pruned it anyway and shall wait and see but it looks a bit lopsided.

The dark lavender cutting looks healthy but it is a slow grower. I mentally, plant, regroup, add, discard as I work. It is a great time too for writing letters in my head and these are so much better than the ones I actually pen!

(Rather like the mot juste you create after the moment has gone)! Angry letters too . . . in my head I get it just right and ram the point home with flair. In fact the written version seems to turn out much less emphatic and not so clearly thought out. The act of gardening obviously has a beneficial effect on one's grey matter.

Friday

To protect our poor M1 pathway James has put a wheelbarrow on its side speared to the ground with a wooden stake. This is in hopes that "they" will use the other path and give this one a well-earned rest. The gulley is very deep now with all the wet and wear and this barring seems the only solution.

Alf has done a similar thing with the car park area, where the once grassy part is all squelchy and spongey with rain, puddled and muddy from tyre-tracks. He has filled six big plastic sacks and positioned them in a row as a marker for a no-go part, reinforced with metal stakes linked with bright yellow plastic tape. It is pretty clear anyway and should, hopefully "Keep the silly buggers off!" for a bit.

Saturday
Our respective bills for the plots have arrived, for next year. Officially we run three plots, two in James' name, one in mine. However as I am an accepted "pensioner" I get a discount, James has to wait a year or two which seems most discriminating! We plan to reverse tenancy this time and I'll have the double one.

★ ★ ★

Digging nearly done for the moment. More parsnips to harvest and the leeks are fattening up.

Cold damp days. The Sunday before Christmas we shall all be invited up to the shed for a drink to celebrate. Not many come but it is a nice idea. Wish we could return to the days when any excuse was made for a bunfight . . . Jubilees; Halloween; Royal weddings, but the social side of our site seems to have lapsed. Maybe Alf will have some of his bright ideas to improve matters. Years ago on every Sunday morning, a bell (since stolen alas), would be rung at eleven o'clock or thereabouts, and tea was served for a couple of pence. It was done on a rota system and worked well but somehow it got lost in the changes of lifestyle, reasons for being there, lack of commitment. Maybe it will return.

At our Sunday Christmas gathering this year, the warm mince pies were distributed by the Hon. Sec.'s amiable lady while he sat in another part of the shed taking orders for seed potatoes, a glass of wine in his hand and a flush on his cheek. In the back area among the smells of peat, compost and damp walls the chaps poured out the red and white, and sherry too, for any who troubled to leave their work and come and join their fellow allotmenteers. The tiny mince pies were ideal, being one-bite sized ones, perfect for earthy hands.

★ ★ ★

I don't suppose we shall be up the plot again this year. It has been the usual mixture of good, bad and indifferent, but always compensatory, always worthwhile. Next year will bring a whole new pattern of growth, produce, with disappointments, nice and nasty surprises, rewards and punishments. It is never the true 'end' of a year on the plot, nor the beginning of the next, rather a rounded affair from season to season. So we order our potatoes, harvest our leeks and mull over the seed packets, putting in and taking out . . . "all the year round".

Other titles in the
Ulverscroft Large Print Series:

TO FIGHT THE WILD
Rod Ansell and Rachel Percy

Lost in uncharted Australian bush, Rod Ansell survived by hunting and trapping wild animals, improvising shelter and using all the bushman's skills he knew.

COROMANDEL
Pat Barr

India in the 1830s is a hot, uncomfortable place, where the East India Company still rules. Amelia and her new husband find themselves caught up in the animosities which seethe between the old order and the new.

THE SMALL PARTY
Lillian Beckwith

A frightening journey to safety begins for Ruth and her small party as their island is caught up in the dangers of armed insurrection.

THE WILDERNESS WALK
Sheila Bishop

Stifling unpleasant memories of a misbegotten romance in Cleave with Lord Francis Aubrey, Lavinia goes on holiday there with her sister. The two women are thrust into a romantic intrigue involving none other than Lord Francis.

THE RELUCTANT GUEST
Rosalind Brett

Ann Calvert went to spend a month on a South African farm with Theo Borland and his sister. They both proved to be different from her first idea of them, and there was Storr Peterson — the most disturbing man she had ever met.

ONE ENCHANTED SUMMER
Anne Tedlock Brooks

A tale of mystery and romance and a girl who found both during one enchanted summer.